Researching
and Writing
in History

Researching and Writing in History

A Practical
Handbook for
Students

by F. N. McCOY

UNIVERSITY OF CALIFORNIA PRESS
BERKELEY / LOS ANGELES / LONDON

University of California Press
Berkeley and Los Angeles, California

University of California Press, Ltd.
London, England

ISBN: 0-520-02447-8
Library of Congress Catalog
Card Number: 73-76110
Designed by Wolfgang Lebrer

Printed in the United States of America

For Joseph A. McGowan

Contents

Preface

THE COLLEGE student's most precious commodity is time. His biggest complaint is that he never has enough of it. This handbook is concerned with time and the term research paper.

Many handbooks on term papers are on the market. In none of them, however, does the author provide the student with directions on the order in which he should use the different library reference tools or with a basis for judgment of just how much time any particular task will take or should take. As a result, libraries remain a mystery; writing and editing remain a chore; the student remains dissatisfied with his finished paper.

In this handbook I have analyzed the stages involved in the term research paper from the viewpoint of the time involved in each, the order in which they should be undertaken, and their distribution over the typical twelve-week college or university quarter. It is written for the history student, whether graduate or undergraduate, or for any student who faces the task of writing a research paper that involves the use of historical tools and the historical method. I have tried not to duplicate material that is available in specialized monographs.

This book grew out of my own experiences as a student and has been enriched by the experiences of my students and what I have learned from them. I wish to express my gratitude for the good humor with which they have submitted themselves to the regime described herein.

I wish to express my gratitude also to Elizabeth K. Nottingham for her encouragement and suggestions and to Gregg Atkins, M.L.S., Librarian at the Law Library of the University of California, Berkeley, and Lecturer in the School of Librarianship, who read the manuscript and made valuable suggestions for its improvement.

1

Introduction

Dᴇᴀʀ ꜱᴛᴜᴅᴇɴᴛ: Welcome to the world of scholarship. Welcome to the exciting, frustrating, and often frightening world of research seminars and research papers, of footnotes and primary sources, of deadlines, and of serious study.

Welcome, also, to a bibliographic world that is out of control and in a state of chaos such as no scientist would have to endure. The historian does not have access to computerized information retrieval systems. His indexes overlap each other in some areas and are incomplete in others. His bibliographies are either a wealth of riches or a big zero.

Be comforted. The historian is a humanist, not a scientist, and the world of the humanist cannot easily be reduced to a strip of computer plastic or punched out on cards. This fact, however, does not excuse the confusion he encounters when he tries to use the university library for research. To the historian, pulling together a bibliography on a subject is like working a jigsaw puzzle with several pieces missing. The puzzle worker, however, has this advantage: he will know, in time, exactly which pieces are missing. The historian can never truly know what is missing from his bibliography because he can never truly know of everything that is available.

The reasons for this confusion are many and real. To begin with, historians are prolific writers. Further, history is an old discipline. Finally, the historian draws upon the sum of man's knowledge in his search for truth. For all these reasons, indexing and classifying material for the historian's use is an overwhelming, if not an impossible, task. For all these reasons, the blame for this confusion does not rest with the librarians. Their job does not include organizing our bibliographic world for us; we who are historians must do it for ourselves. Committees of librarians and historians are in fact working on the problem; the job will not be completed for many years to come, however. For this reason, I have written this handbook. I trust it will serve as a guide in helping you master the world of the professional historian.*

Any guidebook has its limitations, however. It can guide the reader through procedures only up to a point. To that point research is a science, a technique that can be duplicated by any other trained historian. Beyond that point research becomes an art, a sixth sense. It becomes an acquired sensitivity to clues that the researcher will encounter in his reading and involves the willingness to follow up on those clues. Just as the researcher's knowledge of the technique of research will improve with each paper he does, so too will his sense of the art of research improve with each paper.

In the chapters that follow we will guide a student's progress through the researching and writing of one paper, step by step, week by week. For illustration pur-

---

* If you would like to know more about what librarians and historians are doing to help clear up the bibliographic confusion, look into *Bibliography and the Historian: The Conference at Belmont,* Dagmar Horna Perman, ed. (Washington, D.C.: Printed by the Clio Press for the American Historical Association, 1968), 176 pages.

poses, that student is you. For illustration purposes, I have enrolled you in a research seminar in English history. The principles of the search strategy, note taking, evolution of the outline, writing, and editing, however, apply equally well to all topics in history.

Finding a topic

Let us say, for example, that the seminar is on Tudor-Stuart history and that you have a wide choice of possible subjects, everything from the battle of Bosworth to the battle of Blenheim. In the course of that first meeting of the seminar the professor will probably suggest broad subject areas from which the class may choose its topics. Of all those he mentions, perhaps Cromwell appeals most to you. If the professor counsels well, he will say that you must delimit this subject. By this statement he means that you must narrow it down to something you can handle, and complete, in twelve weeks. The most serious error a student makes in the beginning is choosing too large a topic.

A number of ideas will occur to you. If you view Cromwell as something of a dictator, you might think to write a paper comparing him to Hitler. The professor, however, would counsel against this idea. Such a polemic would require years of study. Settle for a topic you can handle. You might think that Cromwell's philosophy of government would be such a topic. The professor, however, would ask whether you have any idea how many volumes are filled with Cromwell's letters, speeches, and papers. Could you possibly go through them all in, say, seven or eight weeks, extracting, analyzing, and synthesizing every statement he ever made on government?

Finding a topic is your first hurdle. About the only

thing you will be sure of at the close of that first seminar meeting is that you do want to write on Oliver Cromwell. Any narrower topic will probably elude you, for the moment anyway.

Knowing this much gives you something to work with. Instead of going home after the seminar is over, go to the library. Look in the author-title card catalog under "Cromwell, Oliver" to acquaint yourself generally with the library's holdings and to find out specifically whether the library has a copy of Cromwell's published letters and speeches. If you find that your library does have a copy, write down the call number and continue browsing through the section on Cromwell for a short biography to read. How will you know which biography to read? As an introduction and overview (which is all you want at this time) almost any biography in a university library will do, and the thinner the better. Go to the stacks; check out that thin biography and check out the collection of Cromwell's writings while you are there. If you wait until tomorrow, someone else might have checked them out before you.

You might return with C. V. Wedgwood's *Life of Cromwell* and with the four volumes of Wilbur C. Abbott's *Writings and Speeches of Oliver Cromwell*. Read Wedgwood quickly that very same night. Do not try to remember all that is in it. You are looking just for ideas.

A wealth of possible topics lies before you. You will probably decide, however, that Cromwell on religion would be too large a topic, as would Cromwell on the Scots. The politics of both the Long Parliament and the Westminster Assembly appear too complicated to handle in only twelve weeks, also. On one page, however, Wedgwood says that Cromwell was "a true believer in liberty of conscience," that he was opposed to the Solemn League and Covenant, and that he therefore only reluctantly signed it. Was Cromwell a liberal? Furthermore, what exactly did the Solemn League and Covenant say that it should be so important? This topic could possibly be a manageable one: Cromwell on the Solemn League and Covenant.

One question remains to be answered: Has Cromwell written enough material on the Covenant for you to write a research paper? Turn to the index in the Abbott collection of Cromwell's writings and look under "Solemn League and Covenant." You will find no listing. Look under "Covenant." You will find a cross-reference to "Covenanters." At this point you may begin to question whether this topic, interesting though it might be, might not be too narrow for you to work on.

Broaden the topic somewhat. If the idea of the Solemn League and Covenant interests you, then perhaps you will want to return to your idea of writing about Cromwell's opinion of the Scots. Check to see what he had to say on that broad subject. Look under "Scotland" in the Abbott collection. You will find many references listed there. Out of this mass of references you should find a suitable topic.

When you left the seminar earlier this same day, you knew only that you wanted to write on Cromwell. Now you have narrowed that subject down to a broad topic: Cromwell on the Scots, or on Scotland. This topic, however, will have to be narrowed down still further.

Ask the professor's advice. The next day tell him what you have read, what your thinking is, and ask his help. In the course of counseling you, he will probably ask about your chief interests. Would you be most interested in Cromwell's attitude toward the Scots government, or in his attitude toward the Scots church, to Scots society, or perhaps to the idea of the incorporation of Scotland with England?

The word "incorporation" may arouse your curiosity. Even the graduate with a year's course in British history behind him is not likely to know much about the attempts of England to join Scotland to it before 1707. The professor's question provides an opportunity to learn something that only the specialist in Anglo-Scots diplomatic relations knows.

Seize the opportunity. If you do, you will have a good working topic for your paper: Cromwell on the union of Scotland with England. You will also have completed the hardest task, finding the working topic. From here on, completing the paper will be just a matter of technique, of budgeting your time wisely, and of self-discipline.

Approaching the research

Now that you have the topic but before you begin the research, stop and ask yourself: What is the purpose of a seminar research paper at this stage in your training, and will that purpose change as you progress further in that training?

First, two of the purposes this paper will not serve: (1) It is not supposed to be just a rehash of what other people have said on the subject; any good freshman can do that; and (2) it is not to be an exposition of your opinion on the subject; few persons are advanced enough for that approach.

At the beginning of the student's professional training, research papers are assigned in order that he can (1) learn something about the variety and locations of source materials, (2) learn how to evaluate source materials, and (3) improve his organizing and writing skills. In short, they are to teach him how to research, analyze, and write. The first purpose teaches the fullest and most efficient use of the library's resources; the second and third purposes teach the student how to think historically and how to write so that he will be read and understood.

All three processes are ongoing. The purpose of the Historical Research Methods seminar is to teach you the fundamentals of research. Each research paper thereafter is a step in learning how to approach the master's thesis, and the purpose of the master's thesis is to test the student's historical skills at the master's level. The thesis, in turn, is only a step toward more detailed and original research papers, and these papers, in turn, are practice for the doctoral dissertation. In short, whether your dissertation eight or nine years from now will be only a hash job or a piece of scholarship will depend largely on how you approach your research on this paper and on how much you learn from it about researching and writing. For these reasons, you have to learn to do it right.

2

Collecting the Bibliography (1):
Start Immediately (*Week 1*)

Two ways of collecting a bibliography are fol-
lowed: the amateur's way and the professional's way.
The amateur's way is the way of the average freshman.
It is to go to the card catalog of the university library
and to use only what is there. It is to find a book or two
listed by one or more of the authors he is reading and to
add that book to the term paper's bibliography. This
method is called the snowball method. It is time-consuming, redundant, and self-limiting. The researcher
who uses this method will never gather together a complete bibliography from which to choose. He will never
develop his knowledge of research reference tools.

The professional does not limit himself to the collection in the university library. He makes use of reference
tools that are in the library's reference room, tools such
as indexes and bibliographies of bibliographies, both of
which reference tools give him a comprehensiveness
that no university library could possibly achieve in its
own collection. In addition, they provide him with a sys-
tematic and relatively thorough method for locating

those materials that his university library does have. After using these tools, the professional researcher makes use of the inter-library loan system. Unfortunately, an inter-library loan takes time, anywhere from a few days to a few weeks. That fact alone is the best reason I can think of for starting on the bibliography immediately.

Be prepared

From this point on, never go anywhere without a pad of 3-by-5-inch notepaper or cards in your pocket. Use them. Never take a bibliographic note on just any old piece of paper you have in your pocket or on a sheet of notebook paper. Use the bibliography cards. Put only one note on a card. Write on one side of the card only.

Be consistent and be thorough. Write your note once and in full and you will not find yourself running back to the card catalog to look up important information that you neglected to write down the first time. Take down the author's name in full, including his middle initial. Write the title in full and the complete information on publisher and date of publication. Copy the number of volumes, if more than one, or the number of pages, if only one volume. Copy down the library's call number. By doing so you will not have to look it up again. All this information, and much more, is given on the catalog card. If you are working from an index, copy the name and year of the particular index in which you found the citation you are taking down. By doing so, you will know exactly where you found that citation. If you find later that you have taken down an incomplete citation, checking up on yourself will be an easier task. An example of a complete note is given below:

Hoffman, W. J.

"Thurloe and the Elections of 1654 and 1656," *Historian* 29: 323-42 (May, 1967)

Biog Index, 1967-70

A color device is useful. I like to use yellow cards for primary sources, green for journal articles, pink for bibliographies, and white cards for secondary book sources. This device is helpful when accidents occur and the cards lie scattered on the floor. It is useful also when you want to grab a section of cards, say those on one type of source only, and you are in a hurry. It is particularly useful when you are typing out the printed bibliography after the paper is finished.

Primary and secondary sources defined

A bibliography divides into at least four categories: (1) primary sources; (2) secondary sources, books; (3) secondary sources, journal literature; (4) bibliographic reference aids, which are also referred to as direct source reference aids.

For the paper on Cromwell, the first primary source is Cromwell himself, what he said and what he did. Other primary sources are available, also. They would be, for example, the diaries of Cromwell's contemporaries, those who worked with him and who were eyewitnesses to what he said and did. Other primary sources would be official government records, the Parliamentary Papers, for example, and the *Acts of the Parliaments of Scotland*. Other types of primary sources, although less reliable for a paper on Cromwell's actions and opinions, would be memoirs written by his contemporaries, or newsletter accounts. In short, the further removed from Cromwell himself or from the years 1649–1658 (that is, from the death of Charles I to the death of Cromwell), the less credible an account would be as a primary source. A primary source would be rendered less credible, also, if the writer were so biased, either in favor of or against Cromwell, as to distort his account beyond a certain degree of latitude. In other words, when a researcher makes use of an individual's written account of a person or of an event, he must investigate the writer of that account. Who was he? What was his relationship to the person or event he was writing about? Where did his interests lie? Answers to these questions will help the researcher to evaluate the credibility of the account.

The secondary sources are the authorities, the historians who wrote and are writing about Cromwell. These sources have a range of reliability, also, and many factors enter into this judgment. Some of these factors are (1) The author's sources: his bibliography should rely heavily upon primary sources rather than upon secondary. (2) His writing: it should be free of loaded or biased words. One noted historian, for example, has written that the Scots ministers were "obsessed with" the Solemn League and Covenant, when a more neutral term would have been "concerned with" or "dedicated to" or even "devoted to." By his choice of the term, "obsessed with," the author revealed his own negative bias; he must be read in this light. (3) The author's credentials or

11

his university affiliation: does he have any? Both are symbolic of scholarly recognition by his peers. (4) The date and place of publication: one would not lend much credence to a history of Roman Catholicism, for example, that was written in the seventeenth century by a Scots Protestant and published in Edinburgh, unedited and unannotated by any later scholar.

In the use of these two kinds of sources, a rule of thumb is this: Never rely on a secondary source if you have access to a primary one. Never cite, that is, never give as a footnote, a secondary source for something Cromwell said or did if you have access to Cromwell's words on the subject. In fact, if you had learned that the university library did not have a collection of Cromwell's speeches and writings and the relevant parts of the Parliamentary Papers as well, you would have had to choose another subject. The historian could not do a research paper on Cromwell's opinions from secondary sources alone.*

The first step:
collecting published bibliographies

The historian's goal in collecting books written about Cromwell and about seventeenth century England and Scotland is to get as complete a list as possible. Although he will not necessarily read every book on his list, the larger the list he collects, the larger the list he will be able to choose from. If he is working on a well-established subject such as Cromwell, he will find that other historians have already compiled good bibliographies on the subject. If he locates these bibliographies,

---

* See Jacques Barzun and Henry F. Graff, *The Modern Researcher,* revised edition (New York: Harcourt, Brace & World, 1970), 430 pages, particularly (for this topic) Chapter 5, "Verification."

he will then have only to complete them, that is, he will have only to add to them the material (books and articles) that has been published since the date of the most recently published bibliography. In order to locate such special bibliographies, he begins by going to a general bibliography of bibliographies, that is, to a book that is a list of books that list books.

General bibliographies of bibliographies

On your first day in the library, immediately after the conference with the professor, begin your search with general bibliographies. Fortunately, many good ones are on the market. The reference librarian should have the following on hand:

> Constance Winchell, *Guide to Reference Books*, 8th ed. (Chicago: American Library Assn., 1967), 3 supplements.
> A. J. Walford, *Guide to Reference Material* (London: The Library Assn., 1966), 3 vols. [Vol. 2 deals with history.]
> Theodore Besterman, *A World Bibliography of Bibliographies*, 4th ed. (Lausanne: Societas Bibliographica, 1965–1966), 5 vols.
> *Bibliographic Index, A Cumulative Bibliography of Bibliographies* (New York: H. W. Wilson Co., 1938–), vol. 1–.

I have listed Winchell first because this bibliography is the one every American college library would have and because any American college or university library would be likely to have most of the books that Winchell lists. On the other hand, Walford is English and is understandably heavy on English bibliographies, many of which would perhaps not be in American libraries. Besterman publishes only those bibliographies that have been published as separate books. It contains no hidden bibliographies as do the others, that is, it contains no bibliographies that form only a part of a larger work. The Wilson *Bibliographic Index,* which is kept up to date by being published three times a year and which cumulates yearly, lists both hidden and separately published bibliographies from 1,700 periodicals as well as from books.

In time you will become familiar with all the general bibliographies of bibliographies I have listed and with others as well. For your present paper, however, this list will suffice, and the place to begin is Winchell.*

In the table of contents of Winchell you will find a section "History and Area Studies" and under that you will find "Europe." Turn to that section and on page 494 you will find the subheading "Great Britain" and under that the subheading "16th and 17th centuries." The first two books listed there are basic to your paper:

> Abbott, Wilbur Cortez. A bibliography of Oliver Cromwell; a list of printed materials relating to Oliver Cromwell, together with a list of portraits and caricatures. Cambridge, Harvard Univ. Pr., 1929. 551p.

---

* Some advisers would have you begin with *Guide to Historical Literature,* George F. Howe, ed. (New York: Macmillan, 1961), which is published under the auspices of the American Historical Association, and which is also found in the reference room. I do not. It is not only out of date, it is highly selective in its listings. Using the system I am about to outline, you will encounter every reference that is in the *Guide,* plus hundreds more. The time will come later in your bibliography collecting to use the *Guide.* That time is not now. If, on the other hand, you wanted only to read a good book on a certain subject and did not mind if that book would possibly be out of date (in research or approach), then the *Guide* would provide a basis for judgment. Starting off with it in the collection of a complete bibliography represents the outmoded hit-or-miss approach to bibliography that is so wasteful of time and energy.

Davies, Godfrey. Stuart period, 1603–1714. Oxford, Clarendon Pr., 1928. 459p. [A volume in the Bibliography of British History series.]

Copy down the full citations, one to each 3-by-5 card. (I would use pink cards for these notes.) The heavy type codes that you see, DC120 and DC121, are Miss Winchell's code numbers for those books. They are not the library's call numbers.

While you have Winchell open, look through the entire section on Great Britain. You may want to take down notes on some of the other books listed there. Under the section "Source Books" you will want to know about the item listed as DC153:

Gardiner, Samuel Rawson. Constitutional documents of the Puritan revolution, 1625–1660. 3rd ed. rev. Oxford, Clarendon Pr., 1906. 476p.

You will need a reliable general history for reference, also. Winchell's DC141 fills that need:

Oxford History of England. 2d ed. Ed. by Sir George Clark. Oxford, Clarendon Pr., 1937–62. [Vol. 9 of this set covers the early Stuart period, 1603–1660.]

Furthermore, since the topic involves Scotland as well as England, you will want to continue browsing through the items listed under "Scotland." Perhaps you could use items DC166, DC168, DC170, or DC172:

Hancock, Philip David. A bibliography of works relating to Scotland, 1916–1950. Edinburgh, Univ. Pr., 1959–1960. 2 v.
New York. Public Library. A list of works relating to Scotland, comp. by George F. Black. N. Y., Lib., 1916. 1233p.

Terry, Charles Sanford. Catalogue of the publications of Scottish historical and kindred clubs and societies, and of the volumes relative to Scottish history issued by His Majesty's Stationery Office, 1780–1908. Glasgow, Maclehose, 1909. 253p.

Dickinson, William Crofts, Donaldon, Gordon and Milne, Isabel A. A source book of Scottish history. London, Nelson, 1952–1954. 3 v.

In taking information from Winchell or any other bibliography of bibliographies, err on the side of copying notes on too many books because you do not know, at this time, which of these books your library has or even which ones you will want to use. If you take notes on only one or two, you may find that your library does not have them in its collection and you will have to return to Winchell and start all over again. In theory, if classifying were uniform and if cataloging were done in depth, the researcher would be able to learn the library's holdings merely by using the card catalog subject headings, that is, by looking under "Great Britain" or "Scotland." Classifying is not uniform, however, and cataloging is not always done either in depth or even correctly to begin with. Therefore, learn to use Winchell to the fullest because, by doing so, you will have the author or editor's name, and even the simplest cataloging system will have an author card as its main entry. If your library has the three paperback supplements to Winchell's 8th edition, be sure to look at them, too, because the cut-off date for books listed in the 8th edition is 1964. The three supplements cover the years 1965 through 1970. Use the supplements in the same way as you used the hardback volume.

A new reference book written just for historians has

appeared recently. *The Historian's Handbook* * offers 300 pages of detailed, organized information about reference works that the historian would use. In Chapter 3, "Guides, Manuals, and Bibliographies of History," Dr. Poulton has a section on Great Britain. One entire chapter is dedicated to "Biographical Materials." Use this new work if your reference librarian has a copy. Browse through it. I did, and in one hour I had collected twelve cards on material on Cromwell and seventeenth century Britain that I had not found in Winchell. These twelve cards included six bibliographies, two primary sources, two nonbibliographic references, and two that I put in the "would like to look into" category.

After you finish with Winchell and Poulton you will have put in approximately two hours in the reference room of the library. In return for those two hours you should have a total of twenty-seven cards: seventeen bibliographies, four primary sources, four nonbibliographic references, and two miscellaneous. You have reached a good stopping place for the day.

However, if you have one hour more at your disposal, you can proceed to the *Bibliographic Index* (also in the reference room) to continue your collection of published bibliographies.

Begin with the most recent volume. Choose certain key words to look under. In the case of a biographical subject, the choice is simplified. "Cromwell, Oliver" is sufficient, although a secondary subject heading could be "Great Britain." Using these key words, work your way backward through the volumes of the *Bibliographic*

* Helen J. Poulton, *The Historian's Handbook: A Descriptive Guide to Reference Works* (Norman, Okla.: University of Oklahoma Press, 1972), 304 pages.

Index to a specific year—set by you—or until you find a bibliography that seems fairly complete.

Your search through this index will be rewarded twice. The first time will be when you learn from the 1971 volume that the bibliography listed by Winchell as DC121 (Godfrey Davies, *Stuart Period, 1603–1660* [Oxford: University Press, 1928], 459 pages) has come out in a new and much expanded edition by Dr. Mary F. Keeler (Oxford, 1970, 734 pages).* The second time will be when you find a bibliographic essay in the 1960–1962 volume:

> Hardacre, P. H. "Writings on Oliver Cromwell since 1929," *J. Mod. Hist.* 33:1–14 (March, 1961).

Both these citations are important finds. Dr. Keeler's book will include material published from the date of the Davies edition in 1928. Hardacre's essay will complete the bibliography by Abbott, which had gone only as far as 1929. Now all you need do is find out what has been published on Cromwell since 1960.

As I went through the *Bibliographic Index* looking for material on the Cromwell topic, I located thirteen citations: four on Cromwell and nine on seventeenth century England. The time required to go through the volumes for 1972 through 1960 and to make complete bibliographic notes on these thirteen citations was only three-quarters of an hour.

---

* If your library was able to supply you with the three supplements to Winchell's 8th edition, you would have learned of Dr. Keeler's new edition of the Davies bibliography by looking in the third supplement, the one that covers the years 1969–1970, under "History—Great Britain—Bibliographies." The descriptive note for the Keeler edition states that her cut-off date is 1962 for books and 1958 for periodicals.

The second step: collecting recent monographs

To find out what has been published on Cromwell since 1960, turn to another of the Wilson indexes, the *Biography Index*. This index pulls together biographical material that has appeared in 1,900 periodicals; it includes books also. It is kept up to date by being published quarterly.

Start with the most recent volume and work your way backward as you did with the *Bibliographic Index*, looking under the heading "Cromwell, Oliver." In another three-quarters of an hour you should be able to collect another twenty-one citations, going back through the volumes to 1958. These twenty-one citations will include sixteen biographies, four articles (including another reference to the Hardacre bibliographic essay), and one biography in a book of biographies.

You now have a good bibliography of material written about Cromwell. Unfortunately, you do not have a complete bibliography. Because of the poor bibliographic control over historical material at the present time, one hundred percent certainty is impossible.

Remember, also, that the *Biography Index* lists only biographical material. You will find nothing indexed here on the related material, nothing on "Scotland" or "Great Britain," for example. Furthermore, if you look at the list of journals that the *Biography Index* indexes, you will find that the *Scottish Historical Review* is not included. You are encountering one of the reasons why one hundred percent certainty in bibliography is impossible to attain. You are encountering an example of an index that is both overlapping and, at the same time, incomplete.

One step more is necessary to complete your search for books about Cromwell, a step that will take five to ten minutes at most. You must cover the months that have intervened since the publication of the last issue of the *Biography Index*. If you are writing this paper during the fall quarter and the month is October, then two months have elapsed since the last issue of the *Biography Index*. Perhaps a book was published on Cromwell in that interval. To find out, go to the *Cumulative Book Index,* which is an index of books published in the English language. It is issued monthly (except August) and is arranged by author, subject, and title. Look under "Cromwell, Oliver" in the issues that have appeared since the publication of the last issue of the *Biography Index*. While you have the *Cumulative Book Index* at hand, look under "Scotland" and "Great Britain" as well.

Whether or not you find anything on any of these topics, you will have the satisfaction of knowing that you have completed a unit of your research; you will know that you have tracked down the secondary book sources on your subject as close to the present as any scholar possibly could.

3

Collecting the Bibliography (2):
Keep at It (*Week 1*)

You NOW HAVE as complete a list of monographs on your topic and subject as you could be expected to collect in the brief time at your disposal. You must still collect "hidden" essays and journal literature. The collection of these parts of the bibliography will be the focus of your third and fourth visits to the library.

The third step: collecting hidden essays

A hidden essay is one that is part of a larger work, a work whose title provides no description of the nature of its contents. For example, a volume might be entitled simply *Essays* and would be a collection of the essays of one author. How would you know without looking at the table of contents what the individual essays were about? Indeed, how would you learn of the existence of the book itself?

The *Essay and General Literature Index* is the key. It is another of the Wilson indexes and is published semiannually. Use this index to find hidden essays on Cromwell, on seventeenth century England, or on seventeenth century Scotland. When you find an essay, be sure to look up (and copy down) the full title, publisher, and publication date of the book that contains the essay; you can do this by turning to the back of the index volume and looking under the heading, "List of Books Indexed."

Taking a 3-by-5 note from the *Essay and General Literature Index* will pose something of a problem in the beginning. You will want to head your card with the author of the essay you are interested in and then put the title of the essay directly under the author's name. This method of note taking could cause you to waste time later on. When you look up the call number, you will be looking for the call number of the book and not of the essay. Furthermore, even if the book is a collection of the essays of one author only, you may find it cataloged under an editor's name. If the book is a collection of essays by different authors, you will definitely find it listed under an editor's name. Resist the temptation, therefore, to put the author of the essay first. An example of a good way to take a note from the *Essay and General Literature Index* is given below.

My examination of this index for the years 1972 through 1955 yielded fourteen citations and required

```
Breen, G. et al.
    The Impact of the Church upon Its Culture:
Reappraisals of the History of Christianity.
Chicago, Univ. Press, 1968.
        (Essays in Divinity, v. 2)

        Contains essay by G.A. Drake "Oliver
Cromwell and the Quest for Religious Toleration," p. 267-291


E & GL Index, 1965-69
```

only three-quarters of an hour. One of those fourteen citations was a note that Hardacre's bibliographic essay had been compiled in a volume, *Changing Views on British History: Essays on Historical Writing since 1929*, edited by E. C. Furber, and published by Harvard University Press in 1966.

When you have completed your search of the *Essay and General Literature Index*, you will have completed your search for published bibliographies, monographs, and essays hidden in larger works. You will have completed your collection of books.

Now is a good time to get the library's call numbers for those books. Separate any cards that bear notes for journal articles—if they are on green cards, the separation process is easy—from the cards that bear notes on books. You should have approximately seventy cards on books. Arrange those cards alphabetically by author or editor. Go to the main card catalog and look up the library's call number for each book.

Interpreting a catalog card

The first card in your bibliography looks like this so far:

```
                              Cromwell : Bibliography

   Abbott, Wilbur Cortez

      A bibliography of Oliver Cromwell; a list of
   printed materials relating to Oliver Cromwell,
   together with a list of portraits and
   caricatures. Cambridge, Harvard Univ. Pr., 1929.

      551 p.



   Winchell
   DC 120
```

The heading at the top, "Cromwell: Bibliography," is your own classification for this card. (Ultimately, you will file this card in your own 3-by-5 file box together with all other bibliographies that you will collect throughout your graduate training. You will, in fact, be compiling your own bibliography of bibliographies.) In the lower left corner you have written "Winchell," indicating where you learned of this book, and Miss Winchell's code, in case you have to look it up again.

When you locate the catalog card in the library, however, you will find that it contains much more information than your card does. The library card will look like this:

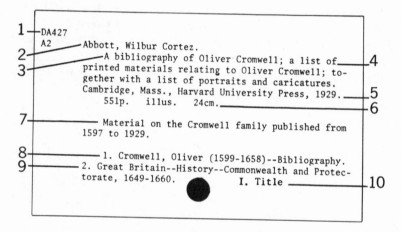

The card shown above is called an *author card;* it is the main entry card. Number 1 is the library's call number. The letters "DA" tell you that the library uses the Library of Congress classification system. If the library used the Dewey system, the call number would begin with a number in the 900s. Number 2 is the name of the author. Occasionally an editor's name will appear here, or if the publication is put out by a branch of the government, rather than by an individual, then the "author" will be that branch of the government. Numbers 3 and 4 are the title and subtitle of the book. Librarians refer to number 5 as the "imprint." The imprint consists of the place of publication, the publisher, and the date of publication. Librarians refer to number 6 as the "collation." The collation gives the number of pages, or volumes, in the work, a statement about illustrations, and the book size. The size of the book is always given in centimeters. This figure is used by the librarian when deciding upon shelving of the volume. If the volume is too large for the regular library shelves, it will have to be placed on special shelves set aside for large volumes.

The number of pages in a book is a good guide to the value of the book relative to your possible use of it and relative, also, to what the book claims to be about. A *History of Great Britain,* for example, that contained only one hundred pages would not be very detailed. In fact, it would be little more than a fast survey of the highpoints in British history. You would not even bother to look at it for the paper you are working on.

Librarians refer to number 7 as a "contents note." A contents note will give you valuable information about the contents of a book. In this case it tells you that Professor Abbott has included material on the Cromwell family as well as on Cromwell himself, and that his collection includes the years 1597 to 1929.

Numbers 8, 9, and 10 are called "tracings." These tracings serve both the librarian and the researcher. They tell the librarian how many cards are in the files (i.e., the card catalog) for this particular book and where those cards are located in the files. If she has to add a note to the main card, she must add it to all the cards. If the volume is lost or destroyed and she removes the main card from the file, she must remove all the cards.

By looking at the tracings, she knows where to go in the files to locate the other cards for this particular book.

The tracings tell the researcher where he might find other material on the particular subject he is studying. The tracings on the Abbott card, for example, advise the researcher to look in the card catalog under "Great Britain—History—Commonwealth and Protectorate, 1649–1660" as well as under "Cromwell, Oliver."

Suppose you had not known about Abbott's book? Could you have found it anyway? The tracings tell you that the library has placed four cards in the author-title card catalog for this particular book. These four cards together give the library user what the librarian calls four "access points," that is, four ways of locating this particular volume: (1) by author, (2) by title, (3–4) by two different subject approaches. If you had looked under "Cromwell, Oliver—Bibliography," you would have located one of these four cards. You would, in fact, have come across the subject heading card referred to by the tracing number 8. This card would look like the author card except that it would have a subject heading typed across the top. (In some libraries this subject heading will be typed in red):

```
        CROMWELL, OLIVER (1599-1658)--BIBLIOGRAPHY
DA427
A2      Abbott, Wilbur Cortez.
            A bibliography of Oliver Cromwell; a list of
        printed materials relating to Oliver Cromwell; to-
        gether with a list of portraits and caricatures.
        Cambridge, Mass., Harvard University Press, 1929.
            551p.   illus.   24cm.

            Material on the Cromwell family published from
        1597 to 1929.

            1. Cromwell, Oliver (1599-1658)--Bibliography.
        2. Great Britain--      History--Commonwealth and
        Protectorate, 1649-     1660.      I. Title.
```

Go through the cards for all the books you have culled from Winchell, Poulton, the *Bibliographic Index, Biography Index, Cumulative Book Index,* and the *Essay and General Literature Index,* copying down the call numbers for each one. The time that this unit of work will require will depend upon the number of books you have accumulated. I spent almost three hours getting call numbers on the seventy-four volumes I had collected and in cross-checking the card catalog when I could not find a book listed under the author or editor.

Study each catalog card as you find it. What bits of information can you pick up from each one? Copy down any contents notes that you find. This information will help you decide which of the books you want to use. A few years from now this information will jog your memory about the book's contents.

If your library appears not to have a certain book, that is, if you cannot find it under the author or editor, look for it under the title. Remember to begin the title with the first concrete word in it, however. Ignore first words such as "A," "An," or "The." Librarians do not include these words in a book's title when they type a title card. If you still cannot find the book, ask the librarian to direct you to the file for books that have been given only temporary cataloging. These books are recent acquisitions. Because the library has not yet received Library of Congress cataloging cards for them, the cataloger has not yet given them their permanent call numbers. You may find cards for one or more of your books in this special file.

Two more clues to follow

The subject heading "Great Britain—History—Commonwealth and Protectorate, 1649–1660" is a clue to the possible existence of a subject heading "Scotland." Pursue that clue while you are at the card catalog and you will find that such a subject heading does exist.* Browse through the books listed there. If the library's holdings are large, you may find cards for C. Sanford Terry, *The Cromwellian Union,* or for C. H. Firth, *Scotland and the Protectorate,* or for C. H. Firth, *Scotland and the Commonwealth,* all published by the Scottish History Society.

Suppose, however, that your library did not have any subject heading for Scotland, or suppose it did not include any of these three volumes in its holdings? How would you learn of their existence? You will learn the answer to this question when you use the published subject bibliographies you found in Winchell and in the *Bibliographic Index.* I cannot stress enough the necessity of using general bibliographies in your research. Do not rely solely upon the holdings of your own library.

The call numbers you have collected provide a second clue to increasing your bibliography. Since all books on any given subject will have call numbers similar to one another, you can browse through the shelves in the areas of the call numbers for the books you have already collected; by doing this you can perhaps add other books to your bibliography. If you do not have access to the stacks, you may still browse through them by using a special card catalog called the "Shelf List." In the Shelf List file all the holdings of the library are filed on cards according to call number, that is, the cards are filed in the boxes in the same order as the books are shelved in

---

* If you would like to investigate the subject of catalog subject headings, ask the reference librarian for the large red volume entitled, *Subject Headings Used in the Dictionary Catalogs of the Library of Congress,* 7th edition (Washington, D.C.: Library of Congress, 1966). This book is a guide for libraries that use the Library of Congress classification system. You can use it to learn what headings relating to your subject are in existence. Their existence, however, does not necessarily mean that your library uses them.

the stacks. This method of browsing is actually superior in many ways to going to the stacks. The shelf list represents the stacks if the stacks were in ideal order, with all books shelved in their right places and none of them checked out. Take the first card in your bibliography (the one for Abbott's collection), browse through the shelf list under the number DA427, and you might find still other bibliographies on Cromwell. Browse through the shelf list under the number DA750 (the first part of the call number for C. Sanford Terry, *The Cromwellian Union*) and you might find still more relevant material published by the Scottish History Society.

Using the *Essay and General Literature Index* and finding call numbers for the bibliography you have collected so far will have required about four hours of work in the library. You have earned the right to call it a day.

4

Collecting the Bibliography (3):
Almost Done (*Week 1*)

THE NEXT unit of work involves tracking down all journal articles that have been published on Great Britain or Scotland since 1960, the date that closed Hardacre's bibliographic essay, or 1958, the date that closed Keeler's collection, and selecting those articles that appear to relate to your broad subject. In the case of these related essays, the date 1960 is an arbitrary one. You may go back to 1950 or 1940 or any date you choose. Beyond a certain date, however, the journal material will have been incorporated in either the bibliographies or the texts of more recent books on the subject. For this reason, I arbitrarily set a ten to fifteen year maximum in searching the journal literature.

The fourth step: collecting journal literature

The essays that appear in the historical journals are usually the results of new research or constitute new twists on old themes. In other words, they usually contain material that has not yet appeared in book form.

Nevertheless, you must show in your research paper that you are aware of, and have read, the latest research on your topic. Therefore, you must search the current literature and bring that search right up to the most recent issue of each of the relevant journals. In addition, you will learn the names of the authorities who are writing currently on your subject. This information will be helpful when you turn to the job of selecting the books you will read.

Hundreds of journals publish articles either on history or on history-related fields. *Ulrich's International Periodicals Directory: A Classified Guide to a Selected List of Current Periodicals, Foreign and Domestic,* which is in the library's reference room, requires twenty-five pages in Volume I to list all the historical journals published around the world. The *Standard Periodical Directory,* also in the reference room, lists Canadian and United States journals and includes history journals. *Historical Periodicals,* also in the reference room, lists journals that regularly publish articles of interest to historians.

Of all the hundreds of journals that are listed by these directories, the beginning scholar should be familiar with the ones most frequently used:

American Historical
   Review
Canadian Historical
   Review
Catholic Historical Review
Church History
Economic History Review
English Historical Review
History
Journal of American
   History

Journal of Medieval and
   Renaissance Studies
Journal of Modern History
Journal of the History
   of Ideas
Journal of Southern
   History
Notes and Queries
Pacific Historical Review
Past and Present
Renaissance Quarterly

Scottish Historical	Sixteenth Century
Review	Journal
Seventeenth Century	Speculum
News	

Incidentally, in the jargon of the librarian, a journal is called a "serial." A serial is a publication that is issued on a regular basis, usually under one generic name. Magazines such as *Time* and *Newsweek* are serials to both the librarian and the scholar; the scholar, however, does not call them journals. A journal is a serial that publishes scholarly articles and reviews books of scholarly interest to those engaged in a particular discipline.

As you read down the list of journals given above, you might have concluded that essays for your paper on Cromwell would most likely be in the *Journal of Modern History*, the *English Historical Review*, the *Scottish Historical Review*, and the *American Historical Review*. Fortunately, you do not have to thumb through all the issues of all these journals in order to locate articles on Cromwell, on the Tender of Union, or on seventeenth century Scotland or England. That work has been done for you and has been compiled in indexes.

First, however, you should know how to find out which journals are handled by which indexes. To learn that, ask the reference librarian for a copy of *Ulrich's International Periodical Directory*, which began publication in 1932 and is issued now in two volumes. The reference librarian will show you how to use these volumes to locate the indexes you will want to use. You will learn that the *Scottish Historical Review* is indexed in the *British Humanities Index*, that the *English Historical Review* is indexed both in the *British Humanities Index* and in the *Social Sciences and Humanities Index*, that the *Journal of Modern History* is also indexed in the *Social Sciences and Humanities Index*, and that the *American Historical Review*

is indexed in the *Readers' Guide to Periodical Literature.*
You are encountering another example of indexes that
are both incomplete and, at the same time, overlapping.

In time you will learn which index deals with which
journals. For now, however, write down this information on one of your green 3-by-5 cards:

```
                                    Indexes to Journals


   AHR  indexed  in  Readers' Guide

   SHR    "    "  British Humanities Index

   EHR    "    "    "         "        "

    "     "    "  Social Sciences & Humanities Index

   JMH    "    "    "    "      "      "      "
```

By doing this, you will be able to bypass having to look
up this information in *Ulrich's* the next time you want to
search the literature in any of these journals.

The journal indexes

Go to the most recent issue of one of the indexes on
your list, to the *Social Sciences and Humanities Index,* for
instance. (These volumes will be in the Reference
Room.) Decide upon certain key words you will look
under, words such as "Great Britain: Civil Wars,"
"Great Britain: Commonwealth" or "Interregnum," and
"Scotland." Look under "Cromwell, Oliver" as well,
even though you should have been able to pick up all
biographical essays in the *Biography Index,* because occasionally you will find some biographical essays that

were not included in the *Biography Index*. (I found two.)

Starting with the most recent issue, look under all these key words. When you find any articles that appear to relate to your topic or period, copy down a complete bibliographic note, each note on a separate green 3-by-5 card. Notice that you will find articles indexed from journals other than the *English Historical Review* and the *Journal of Modern History*. You may find relevant essays from *Encounter* and from *History* as well.

Work your way backward in the issues of the index, looking up articles under the key terms you have chosen. As you do so, you will notice that the index appears to stop with the year 1965. Not really. In that year the index was first published under its current title. Before 1965 its name was the *International Index: A Guide to Periodic Literature in the Social Sciences and Humanities*. Continue working your way backward through the *International Index* until you have completed your search.

In the 1960–1962 volume you will encounter a fourth reference to Hardacre's bibliographic essay. It is listed in this index because it appeared in the *Journal of Modern History*, which is indexed by the *Social Sciences and Humanities Index*. It appeared in the *Essay and General Literature Index* because the essay had been included in a volume of essays about British history and had thus become hidden. It appeared in the *Biography Index* because it is about a biographical subject. Finally, it appeared in the *Bibliographic Index* because it is a bibliographic essay. With the finding once again of this essay, you need go no further in the *Social Sciences and Humanities Index*. From the volumes that cover the years 1973 through 1960 you should have been able to glean twenty-two citations; the time involved should have been no more than one and one-quarter hours.

Turn to the second index on your list, the *Readers' Guide to Periodical Literature*, and repeat the process. In this index you will find articles indexed from the oldest history journal in the United States, the *American Historical Review.* The *A.H.R.* is in this index, along with articles from *Ladies' Home Journal* and *McCall's,* because it is such an old journal, although a more commonsense classification would place it in the *Social Sciences and Humanities Index.* Searching through the issues of the *Readers' Guide* back through 1959 should take no longer than half an hour and should yield six citations: three articles and three book reviews.

The last index to be examined is the *British Humanities Index,* where you will find articles indexed from the *Scottish Historical Review.* Searching through this index will require about two hours because its classification is detailed. If I were doing this paper, I would look under the following headings: (1) Civil War, (2) Cromwell, Oliver, (3) England—History, (4) Great Britain—History—17th century, (5) Great Britain—Parliament—Commons—History, (6) Great Britain—Parliament—History, and (7) Scotland—History. I found that by following up on all the cross-references that were listed under these headings, I was able to add sixteen citations to my bibliography, using the volumes of the *British Humanities Index* back through 1960.

You will find that this index, too, had two names. From its beginning in 1915 through 1961 it was called the *Subject Index to Periodicals.* With the 1962 volume it was given its current name.

When you have finished with these three indexes and have eliminated all duplications, you should have four dozen green 3-by-5 cards, each one of which bears a bibliographic note on a different article that has appeared since 1960 on Cromwell, England, Scotland, or Anglo-Scots relations in the seventeenth century. As you make these notes you will notice that certain authors' names will have appeared on more than one article. In this way you will begin to familiarize yourself with the names of the persons who are currently doing research on your topic and subject.

As you finish your search through each index, make a note to yourself on one of your 3-by-5 cards to that effect. For example, "S.S. & H. Index: 1973–1960, done." By doing this, you relieve yourself of the necessity of having to remember this bit of clerical information. In addition, you will be able to check later on your thoroughness.

In four hours you will have made a search of the current literature up to the date of publication of the last issue of the different indexes. You will now have to examine the most recent issue of each of the journals in which you found articles listed. This step is necessary because publication of the indexes does not necessarily coincide with the publication of the journals, and, as a result, the indexes may lag behind the journals by one or even two issues.

Journals are shelved usually in two places in the library. The older issues, those that have been bound in annual or biennial cumulations, will be in the stacks together with the other books on the same subject. The issues for the current year, however, will be in the periodicals room. They will be unbound, and the classification and shelving will vary from one college to another.

You will require one hour, approximately, to examine the most recent issue of each journal that is important to your paper. If you bog down in browsing—as historians tend to do—you could take all day. As with your use of the *Cumulative Book Index,* however, whether or not you find anything, you will have the satisfaction of having done a thorough piece of work. No one could have done it better.

5

Collecting the Bibliography (4):

A Job Well Done (*Week 1*)

W<small>HEN</small> <small>YOU</small> return to the library the following day
you will examine the bibliographies you found in Win-
chell, Poulton, and the *Bibliographic Index*. After you
have visited the stacks and finally have the bibliographies on the carrel desk before you, you might be
tempted to put them down and lull yourself into the
idea that you have collected your bibliography. Not so.
All you have are lists of books, hundreds of them. You
must cull your bibliography from them. This unit of
work can take as long as you want it to. For the sake of
expediency, however, set yourself a time limit of, say,
three to four hours and try to stay within it.

The fifth step: selecting your books

In selecting secondary sources you will be confronted
with the necessity of making choices. You cannot read
them all in the time you have at your disposal. You must
decide which books on the lists are pertinent to your
theme and which are not. Which books are worth reading in full and which should only be scanned? Which
books will you need as auxiliary reference sources?

Several guidelines can be drawn to help you make these decisions. Let your theme be a guide. You would certainly want to include any book whose title or table of contents indicated that it dealt largely with Cromwell on Scotland. Let the name of the publisher be another guide. The scholarly books are published usually by the large university presses: Oxford and Cambridge in England; St. Andrews and Edinburgh in Scotland; Harvard, Yale, Princeton, Chicago, California (as examples) in the U.S.A. Books written for the layman are published usually by the commercial publishing houses. This fact does not mean that they are not good; it may mean only that the books have wide commercial appeal but are nevertheless based on sound scholarship. Avoid those books that are privately printed, in the twentieth century at least. Let the decade in which the book was published be another guide. As a rule of thumb, historical interpretations underwent revision following World War II and again in the 1960s. This fact does not mean that earlier interpretations are wrong; it means only that they are different. A good policy to follow would be to choose one book from each of the decades of the twentieth century.* No rule, however, says you may not choose more. Let the size of the book, in relation both to its title and to your use of it, be another guide. I would question the completeness of Professor Abbott's bibliography if, covering a period of more than three hundred years, it contained only one or two hundred pages. Its five hundred and fifty-one pages, however, tell me that this volume is, indeed, a thorough one.

How thorough were you when you were working

---

* The A.H.A. *Guide to Historical Literature,* referred to on p. 14, could be of help here in guiding your selection from among the many books that were published in the twentieth century prior to 1960. Used for this purpose and at this step in your bibliography collecting, the *Guide* is helpful.

with Winchell? Did you make bibliographic notes on items DC170 and DC171? If you did, and if you were able to locate either or both of these bibliographies in your library, you would be learning now about the existence of the volumes I referred to earlier: *The Cromwellian Union, Scotland and the Protectorate,* and *Scotland and the Commonwealth.* You would be learning also of the existence of a long series of monographs published by the Scottish History Society. If your library did not have this collection among its holdings, and you had relied solely upon the card catalog, you would have missed them entirely; you would have missed an invaluable source of primary material.

After you have spent three to four hours culling your primary and secondary sources from the published bibliographies, arrange your note cards alphabetically by author or editor and go to the card catalog to learn how many of these books your library has in its collection. Copy down the call numbers on the individual cards.

Before you leave the library this day, take out several of the books in your bibliography. Choose the ones that you know you must use.

One day more

If you found that your library does not have all the books on your list, and it undoubtedly will not, now is a good time to make use of the inter-library loan desk. Which books will you order? No one can make that decision for you. In the case of secondary sources, however, the book reviews will help you decide.

The sixth step: locating book reviews

Book reviews are usually found in the journals. To locate book reviews you must go first to the book review indexes. They will tell you in which volume of which journal a review will be found. The reference librarian should have the following book review indexes on hand:

> *Book Review Digest* (New York: H. W. Wilson Co., 1905—).
> *Index to Book Reviews in the Humanities* (Detroit: Philip Thomson, 1960—). Only English language periodicals are indexed.
> *Book Review Index* (Detroit: Gale Research Co., 1965—).

In order to use these indexes you must know the date of publication of the book you are interested in because reviews are published around the time of the book's publication. You must know, also, which of the book review indexes to use. To know this, you must know when each of the book review indexes began publication. For example, you would not be able to find the original review for Wedgwood's *Life of Cromwell* (which was first published in 1939) in the *Book Review Index* because the *Book Review Index* did not start publication until 1965.

The back issues of the journals (to which the book review index will direct you) will usually be in the stacks. You will find the call numbers for these bound journals in the card catalog, under the title of the journal. In some libraries a list of the library's journal holdings is kept in a separate file in the reference room near the indexes. This list will also give you the journal call numbers.

When you locate a reference to a book review, copy down the information on the same 3-by-5 card on which you took the original bibliographic note. Each one of your book cards will now be a complete record of all the information you need on each book. Each card will contain a complete bibliographic citation, the library's call number for the book, the location of reviews of the book, and the call numbers for the journals where the reviews may be found. An example of a complete note card is given below:

```
DA     Hill, Christopher
H49         God's Englishman; Oliver Cromwell and the
1970   English Revolution. New York, Dial Press, 1970.

       324 p. Bibliography
            Crosscurrents in World History Series

       Book Review Digest, 1970
       Reviews:  Library J  95:2662 (Aug. 1970) [Lib. Schl.]
                 N.Y. Times Bk. R. (Oct. 4, 1970) [AG N73]


Biog Index, 1970-71
```

A good idea is to copy the call numbers for the journals a second time, on the card on which you noted where the journals are indexed. On one card you will now have all the information you need to locate a journal in the stacks and also to locate an index to its articles. For example:

```
                                  Indexes to Journals


[AG/A48] AHR indexed in Readers' Guide

[DA750/S2] SHR    "    "    British Humanities Index

[AG/E5] EHR       "    "    "        "        "

              "   "    "  Social Sciences + Humanities Index
[DI/J6] JMH       "    "    "    "    "    "    "
```

Go to the bound journals in the stacks and read the reviews on the books that your library does not have. Let the tenor of the review determine whether you will place an inter-library loan order. After you have read the reviews and have determined which books you want to use, place your order immediately. Remember, several weeks could pass before the books arrive.

Choosing among different editions

Sometimes a scholar will compile an edition of primary source material when another edition is available. The material will be substantively the same; the editorial interpretation will differ. Cromwell's writings are a case in point. At the card catalog, under "Cromwell, Oliver," you learned that the library has two different collections of Cromwell's writings. One collection was made by Thomas Carlyle in the nineteenth century; one collection was made by Wilbur Abbott in the twentieth century. Which should you choose as your basic reading? Hardacre's excellent bibliographic essay should have given you a guide in this matter, but suppose you do not care to take his word for it? Suppose you had no such guide? In that case you must have bases on which to make a decision.

The criteria are essentially the same as those used in evaluating any other book. You have already taken out the Abbott collection and have used it; you are familiar with its format. Examine the Carlyle collection now. Let the prose of the editor's commentary be a guide. You will realize that the style of Carlyle is rhetorical, whereas that of Abbott is historical. Look at the footnotes: which collection contains more scholarly annotations? What were Carlyle's credentials? Who was Abbott? (You will find this information either on the title page or in the preface.) For the historian, the Abbott collection is superior on all counts, although for a student of literature the Carlyle collection might be preferred. Can you use the Carlyle collection? Yes, if you decide to include in your paper a section on the historiography of the subject. If you do, you will undoubtedly wish to include Carlyle in his capacity as a nineteenth century historian. For your basic reading, however, Abbott is the preferred edition.

A checklist on your thoroughness

If you have been following the suggested schedule, you should have been able to collect your basic bibliography in seventeen to twenty hours divided over seven days. Although you will add to your bibliography as you read, by the time the seminar meets the second week, you will have chosen your topic and collected the bulk of your bibliography as well. Use the following checklist to test your thoroughness:

MONDAY: First meeting of the seminar.
   (1) Choose your subject.
   (2) Read a short biography.
TUESDAY: Have a conference with the professor.
   (1) Choose a working topic.
   (2) Go to the library.
     Step 1: Collect published bibliographies:
       (a) Winchell, *Guide to Reference Books* (1 hour).
       (b) Poulton, *The Historian's Handbook* (1 hour).
WEDNESDAY: Finish Step 1:
       (c) *Bibliographic Index* (¾ hour).
     Step 2: Collect recent monographs.
       (a) *Biography Index* (¾ hour).
       (b) *Cumulative Book Index* (10 minutes).

THURSDAY:

> *Step 3:* Collect hidden essays, using the *Essay and General Literature Index* (¾ hour).

> Get library call numbers on books (2–3 hours).

FRIDAY:

> *Step 4:* Collect journal literature:
> > (a) *Social Sciences and Humanities Index* (1¼ hour).
> > (b) *Readers' Guide to Periodical Literature* (½ hour).

SATURDAY: Finish step 4:

> > (c) *British Humanities Index* (2 hours).

> Examine the most recent issue of all relevant journals (1 hour).

SUNDAY:

> *Step 5:* Select your books (3–4 hours):
> Get the library call numbers for each book.
> Charge out the most important ones.

MONDAY:

> *Step 6:* Locate book reviews (¾ hour):
> > (a) *Book Review Digest*
> > (b) *Index to Book Reviews in the Humanities*
> > (c) *Book Review Index*

> Read book reviews (1 hour).
> Put in inter-library loan order.

MONDAY: Second meeting of the seminar.

Where do you go from here?

Before you start your serious reading and note taking, you have one essential step to go through. It is the browsing period, the breathing space between two units of concentrated work. Take a couple of evenings and browse through Abbott's four volumes. Learn his organization of the material. Familiarize yourself with

Cromwell's style and with Abbott's as well. Browse through the other books you have charged out of the library.

This browsing period is essential for a humanist. It is one of the ways whereby you will be able to make the transition to the period you are studying, and that mental transition is essential in order to develop the empathy the historian must have.

As you browse, certain questions will come to mind. Write them down on one or more 5-by-8 note cards. Who exactly was Cromwell? During what years was he active in public life? What exactly was his job? How did he get it? What was the Tender of Union? Who proposed it? When was it written? Why? Who wrote it? Under what circumstances? What exactly did it say? What did it *not* say? How did the Scots magistrates react to it? Did they react alike? If not, why not?

You will have to answer all these questions, and many more, before you will be in a position to ask and answer the final one: what was Cromwell's attitude toward the Union? Furthermore, you will have to know everything he said or wrote on the subject (everything that was recorded, anyway) before you can begin to try to answer the really unanswerable question: why did he hold that opinion?

As you make out this list you will notice that you are in fact beginning to make a rough outline for your paper. You are asking the questions you will have to answer in the writing of your paper. You will be on your way.

6

Reading and Note Taking:
Organization Is the Key (*Weeks 2–7*)

WHEN YOU do not know how to begin, sharpen all your pencils. Much good can be accomplished by preparing mentally for a job of work, by putting your desk in order, by buying the equipment you will need, by organizing. These activities are, in fact, essential to doing a good job. They provide percolating time.

Organize your equipment

As a serious student, you will need basic equipment for your research. Buy it now; it will not be any cheaper next year. You will need a card box to hold 3-by-5 bibliography cards, a card box to hold 5-by-8 note cards, and a file box (9-by-12 inches) to hold class notes, term papers, and the many printed bibliographies you will collect during your years in graduate school. You will need manila folders, pads of 3-by-5 paper or cards, pads of 5-by-8 note paper or cards, and white and yellow typing paper. I buy both yellow and white 5-by-8 cards or pads of paper for taking notes: white for secondary sources and yellow for primary. This device helps me tell at a glance how many notes I am piling up from each kind of source. You will need dividing cards for these file boxes also. Buy plain ones rather than those with headings printed on them. You will be making your own categories. Even at this early stage in your research you have three different categories for the 3-by-5 card box: primary; secondary, books; and secondary, journals. Write the headings in pencil; you may want to change them later.

Organize your time

The moment of truth has come. How much study can you take at any one sitting? If differs with different people. If you allow six weeks for reading and researching your paper, make a schedule of your duties over that period of time. Set aside on that written schedule a certain number of hours each week for work on your paper, for example, three hours each on Monday, Wednesday, and Friday, and four hours on Saturday morning.

Be realistic when you are making out a schedule. Allow for human weakness, but not too much. Give yourself plenty of free coffee time, but do not overdo it. If possible, set aside the same time of day every day and stick to it. Do not try to cover too much ground in any one day. Two to three hours a day of concentrated work will add up. The momentum will build up gradually as your interest in the subject develops and as your understanding of its intricacies increases. Within a week or two you will have built up your staying power to where you will be able to handle three to four hours of research a day. To sum up: make a realistic schedule tailored to your needs and stick to it.

Organize your notes

Learning to take research notes is an art. How much do you copy down? What is important? Do you copy exactly or paraphrase? I tell my students not to take notes beginning with page one of any book they are reading. Read further. You may not get the gist of an author's theme until you are into that book some twenty or even thirty pages. When you do realize the direction the author is taking, you can always go back to page one, reread those early pages quickly, and on that second reading you will know what is important because you will know where the author is going. Sometimes you will sense that something you are reading might be important, but you do not know for certain how it will fit in. In that case, make a direct quote from your source and below it write your impression of how you think you might be able to use it. Sometimes you will not understand a page of text. In that case, make a note to yourself on a 5-by-8 card, citing the source and page, and tell yourself, "Do not understand; must read again. Something about internal dissention between two Scots groups—Protesters and Resolutioners—regarding the Union. Who were these?"

In determining how long a note you should take, let your guide be the size of the note paper: 5-by-8 inches. Let your note be no longer than that which you can write on one side only. Never write on the other side. You will probably forget that you *have* written on the other side. Even if you do remember, when you come to making your outline, you will not be able to scan all your material in one glance. Some of it will be out of sight, hence out of mind. If you must take a note or write out a flash of insight that takes more than one card, continue that note or thought on a second card.

Each card should have a format, and that format should be consistent. I code each card in the upper left corner with a subject. For example, some subjects for this paper would be "Cromwell: on the Scots Parliament, 1650" or "Glasgow's refusal to sign, 1652." On matters of opinion I always write down a date as part of the code because opinions change with time. If I do not record when and under what conditions a person gave his opinion on a matter, all I will have (when I start to make an outline) will be a hodgepodge of quotes with no potential for historical use.

Whenever you write down a quote, put it in quotation marks. Using this device, you will never have to wonder later whether that statement was something you took from a book or something you thought up. Remember, you do not want to run the risk of even unintentional plagiarism. Under the quote write a note to yourself, or whatever synthesis you can make, or the question the quote raises in your mind.

Remember to cite your source directly on your note card. I do this at the bottom of the card. You need not write down the complete bibliographical note, or even the complete title. You will develop your own shorthand for this citation, but be consistent. A typical note citation for this paper could read, "Abbott, Writings, IV, 794," which translates to "Abbott, *Writings and Speeches of Oliver Cromwell,* vol. IV, p. 794" or "Terry, Cr. Union, 15," which translates to "Terry, *The Cromwellian Union,* p. 15."

At first you may not know how to arrange your cards in the box. That knowledge, too, will come within a brief time. If you go over your notes regularly, every few days, they will begin, gradually, to form themselves into groups. Within a week or two you will know of certain headings you will want to write on your 5-by-8 dividing cards. "On Leslie" will be one; "On the Tender" will be another. "On Universities," "On the General Assembly" will be others. Within only a couple of weeks you will be gratified to notice how your notes will have accumulated and you will be proud of the well-organized condition they will be in. In note taking, neatness counts. You will save time later.

Organize your approach

When you are starting your reading on any subject, do you begin with the primary or with the secondary sources? If you begin with the secondary, do you begin with the books or with the journal articles? The choice is yours. You can go either (1) directly to the primary sources, study them, and form your own conclusions, or (2) directly to the secondary sources, read what they have to say, and turn afterward to the primary sources.

Each method has its own advantages and disadvantages. If one of the reasons for assigning research papers is to give the student the opportunity to learn how to evaluate for himself, however, rather than take other people's conclusions as his own opinions, the first method would be the one that would train your analytical abilities. With the second approach you could have your opinions formed for you. Your attitude could be colored in advance, as you approach the primary sources, by what the authorities have had to say.

The second approach is much easier. The first approach, however, will pay bigger dividends in the years to come, but it is time-consuming; you will have to read the same statement or page over and over, as you try to pull from it all that it contains and integrate it with your other notes. The second approach, however, is the undergraduate's way; the first approach is the professional's way.

For your first paper, perhaps you should try a middle course. You have read one short biography of Cromwell. I suggest that you read another one in your bibliography, one of Maurice Ashley's biographies of Cromwell, for example. Then turn to your chief primary source: Cromwell's *Writings.* You do not have to read all four volumes; use the index. Read what he had to say about the topics that are important to your paper. Each topic will refer you to another in these volumes. Take down your notes as I have suggested. When you have worked each day for the period of time you set aside for yourself, stop. If you do not, you run the risk of over-doing one day and of doing nothing the next day. Slow and steady is a better way.

If you have set aside six weeks for research, a reasonable breakdown of your use of the sources would be to spend three weeks on your primary sources and three weeks on your secondary ones. Therefore, after you have worked with Cromwell's *Writings* for about a week, turn to your other primary sources. Spend a week or more with them. Study the wording of the Tender and the parliamentary acts for references to it. Read Terry's collection of documents to learn what the Scots thought about it. After you have begun to form your own conclusions, spend one or two evenings writing down your impressions. Remember, however, that these conclusions are only tentative and are based upon the understanding that you have at this stage in your research.

Turn, then, to the secondary sources. Read what the historians have said on the subject. Study their arguments. If any one or all of them disagree with the conclusions you have reached, return to the bases for your own conclusions and develop them again. Then go back to the authorities. Try to refute their conclusions, basing your argument always on the primary sources, on what Cromwell himself said or did, and on the wording of the Tender itself.

You may learn, however, that the authorities agree with you. Notice the way I have phrased that: they agree with you. Some students are discouraged when they learn that a conclusion they have derived for themselves through hard work is not new. What a silly way to react! Instead, they should be gratified, and perhaps a bit proud, to realize that the authorities on the subject have come to the same conclusion. That fact does not take away from the fact that *you* came to that conclusion on your own, without any help from them. The discovery that the authorities agree with you means only that you are developing the ability to reach a sound historical conclusion on your own. This ability is the one you will need if you are some day to write a good master's thesis or a first-rate doctoral dissertation, at which time you will be working on an original topic, at which time *you* will be the authority, and perhaps the only one.

If they do not agree with you, and you believe that you can substantiate your conclusions from the primary sources, do not be afraid to do so. Do not become emotional in your writing, however, and do not go off on a tangent. I shall have more to say about this topic in Chapter 9, on writing.

If, on the other hand, the authorities differ from you and you cannot refute them and yet you cannot agree with them, the time has come for you to study and evaluate yourself, your own biases, perhaps even your own limitations.

After you have spent two weeks on your secondary sources (books), and after you have compared their conclusions with yours, turn to the journal articles and spend a week on them. Perhaps you will find that one of these historians agrees with you. If so, is it on the same basis? If he disagrees with one of your book sources, in what respect? On what basis? Is his basis sound? You have read Cromwell; you have your own basis for judgment. You do not have to accept the historian's conclusions. Return always to the primary sources. The answers lie there.

If you change direction

During the course of your reading you may have found yourself deviating from your original topic. Perhaps your interest and reading veered in the direction of the reaction of the Scots magistrates (or writers or church leaders) to the Tender of Union. Perhaps you became more involved with the English Parliament, with its composition and the attitudes of its members toward the subject of union. Indeed, perhaps you were not able to find enough primary and secondary material on Cromwell on the subject of the Union. Perhaps you found yourself becoming increasingly interested in the problem of union that existed throughout the entire seventeenth century, with Cromwell's attempt at union becoming only one solution to that problem.

If you find that your notes have been veering away from the topic originally agreed upon, you should be bringing out this fact in conferences with the professor. A change in direction from the original working topic is permitted when that change is the result of research; indeed, such a change is common. Keep the professor informed of such changes as you work with the sources, however. Do not surprise him at the end of the quarter with a finished paper that is substantively different from the working topic you both agreed to at the beginning of the quarter.

When you come to the end of the six-week period you set aside for your research, stop. This act is one of pure self-discipline, because no historian believes that he has ever collected enough material. A pile of unread books will always remain, a treasure of unsampled sources. Nevertheless, stop! My master professor used to say, "There's a time to stop reading and start writing." That time has come for you now. If you have been following the schedule I suggested, you have more than enough material to write about, although if you *have* been following that schedule, you are undoubtedly convinced at this point that you know nothing. That sign is a very hopeful one.

7

Other Reference Aids:

The Professional Uses Them (*Weeks 2–7*)

As you study the sources certain questions will come to mind, questions that the sources will not be able to answer. You will have to turn to other reference aids.

I have referred you thus far to indexes, to bibliographies of bibliographies, and to specialized bibliographies. These volumes represent one form of reference tool. The librarian calls them "bibliographic" reference works or "indirect sources." They are books that list titles of books or articles; they give information about literature in one form or another.

A second kind of reference tool is in the university library. The librarian refers to these volumes as "nonbibliographic" reference works or "direct sources." They give information about matters other than literature; hence they are called nonbibliographic. They give information about people, places, things, and events.

Examples of nonbibliographic reference works are the encyclopedia and the dictionary. These sources are the ones every undergraduate knows. The professional knows, and uses, many more. Unfortunately, they are usually in the reference room of the library and do not circulate. You must use them there. Because of this fact, many students ignore them.

As a student-historian you cannot afford to ignore them. As you read through your material you came across certain words: "Leslie," for example, and "Glasgow," "Covenanters," and *"Ne Impune lacessit."* If you are to do an honest job of research, you must know to what or to whom these words refer. You must know more detail, also, than your undergraduate textbook in British history or your dictionary will give you. As you come across these words write them down, each on a separate 5-by-8 card. When you have collected several such cards, go to the reference room and find out what the terms mean. How many cards you should collect before you make your trip to the reference room is up to you. Let your guide be at that point in time when you are no longer able to read your sources with meaning.*

What reference sources will you go to? I could give you a list of nonbibliographic reference aids for this particular paper you are writing, but that list would not necessarily help you with the next research paper you work on. For this reason I refer you again to Winchell's *Guide to Reference Books,* the original hardbound volume and the three paperback supplements. Read the table of contents. Turn to sections other than history. You will find almost everything you need listed somewhere in Winchell. In the list of nonbibliographic reference aids that I shall give below, only two are not listed in Winchell. The code that I have written after the title of each book is Miss Winchell's code for that book. I include

---

* Every serious student should build up his own home reference shelf, one that would be adequate to answer these peripheral—but pertinent—questions. The financial investment will be repaid by your having to make fewer trips to the library. See the Appendix for my personal selection.

these codes in order to demonstrate the many different sections in Winchell that give reference material relating to your paper on Cromwell.

About people

The *Dictionary of National Biography* (AJ144) is truly not a dictionary but is rather a multivolume collection of biographies of dead Britishers. Remember, no living persons are included in the *DNB;* no persons are included who were not British. You will find a biography of Leslie in this reference aid; you will find biographies of other persons named by Cromwell also. *Who's Who in History* (AJ153) also gives biographies. Three volumes have been published to date. The third volume covers the period you are interested in, 1603 to 1714. One of the two volumes that Winchell does not list is Mary F. Keeler's *Members of the Long Parliament, 1640–1641, a biographical study of its members* (1954). You will not understand Cromwell's references to parliamentary members unless you refer either to Dr. Keeler's book or to D. Brunton and D. H. Pennington's *Members of the Long Parliament* (1954).

About places

No historian can be without an atlas. Unless you look up the location of unfamiliar places, how could you understand, for example, the significance of the refusal of Glasgow to agree to the Union? Unless you see for yourself Glasgow's strategic location in West Scotland and thus realize that its refusal could influence one-third of Scotland, you will not understand why the English government took the action it did to persuade Glasgow to agree. Muir's *Historical Atlas* (DA56), Rand McNally's

Atlas of World History (DA58), or Shepherd's *Historical Atlas* (DA59) should be part of the home reference shelf of every student-historian. If you do not own one of these atlases, you will find them in the reference room. Use them.

About things

Your paper deals with four subjects: (1) English constitutional history, (2) Scots constitutional history, (3) English church history, and (4) Scots church history. Most of your sources will expect you to understand the expressions and technical terms that the authors employ. If you do not, you must go to reference aids that will explain them. Malloch's *A Practical Church Dictionary* (BB31) or Purvis's *Dictionary of Ecclesiastical Terms* (BB40) will explain some of the technicalities of Anglican Church language, which you will need to know. Gee and Hardy's *Documents Illustrative of English Church History* (BB55) will fill you in on some of the more important documents pertaining to the English Reformation and the subsequent Puritan movement in England, the movement in which Cromwell was involved. Gardiner's *Constitutional Documents of the Puritan Revolution* (DC153) and Dickinson and Donaldson's *Source Book of Scottish History* (DC172) both give excerpts from texts pertinent to the Union. Gardiner will interpret those texts from the English point of view; Dickinson and Donaldson will give something of the Scots point of view. Cheney's *Handbook of Dates for Students of English History* (DC135) is essential for the person who writes about English history prior to 1752, because before that date England was on the old Julian calendar, whereas most of the continental states, and Scotland also, were on the new Gregorian calendar.

About people, places, things, and events

Encyclopedias are repositories of information on all manner of subjects. Fortunately, many good encyclopedias are on the market. For your paper on England, I suggest that you use the *Encyclopaedia Britannica* (AD2) because it contains more articles on Britain than do other encyclopedias. Use the index because references to any item are often scattered throughout many volumes. Look up "Covenanters" in the encyclopedia. Because your paper deals with ecclesiastical as well as political matters, you might refer also to a specialized encyclopedia such as the *Encyclopedia of Religion and Ethics* (BB12). In this encyclopedia, old but not superseded, you will find material you will not find anywhere else.

When you start writing your paper, you might cite some of these aids. More often, however, the historian consults them only because he will not be able to study his sources meaningfully without using them. The information they contain will help in the interpretation of the primary sources; it will help in the evaluation of the arguments and interpretations of the secondary sources as well. Incidentally, if you find that one of your secondary sources has made an error in fact because he relied on his memory instead of consulting one of these reference aids, you have the making of a good substantive footnote. Correct him, but do it gently.

Regardless of what the subject of your next paper may be, once you have learned how to make full use of Winchell in locating nonbibliographic reference aids, you will be able to adapt that technique to any other topic.

8

Percolating Time:

Use It to Advantage (*Week 8*)

THE WEEK following completion of your research is one of mental organization, of thinking and rethinking the material you have read, of letting the outline take shape in your mind and on paper, of retreat from the real world. It is a week of percolating time.

The metaphysical use

At the metaphysical level this week is one of gathering the tension necessary to perform the creative act of composition. Since every creative act involves a turning inward of the artist upon his own resources, this week should find you so totally involved with what you are about to undertake that you will find yourself involuntarily conserving your energies and withdrawing from the real world into the isolated world of the artist.

You have probably never looked upon the term paper as an act of creation; you have undoubtedly never considered yourself an artist. Nevertheless, such it is and such you are. If you can develop a sense of anticipation, of excitement, over what you are about to create, you will find that your attitude toward term papers will change, and for the better. At the mundane level, your grades will improve. At the level of self-awareness, your need for self-satisfaction will be gratified. You will like your term papers more; you will like yourself more.

This week is one during which you will be in the world but not of it. It is one during which you should perform routine, mechanical tasks that can, and should, be done alone, so that you can be alone with your thoughts. Wash the car. Wax it. Clean out your bureau drawers or your desk. When you turn on the TV, you should find yourself staring at it without actually watching or hearing it because your thoughts will be occupied with your paper. Keep it uppermost in your mind. Do not allow yourself to be distracted from it.

This week is one during which the conversation of others will suddenly become annoying to you. You will be irritated by being distracted from something as important as your paper by something as unimportant as what TV show your best friend watched last night. Avoid that friend. In general, avoid people. This advice applies to spouses as well.

Do not talk to others about your paper. Keep it to yourself. Too many students, and teachers as well, talk themselves out, dissipate the creative tension in conversation and, afterward, when they sit down at the typewriter, they find they have nothing to say because they have said it all. The tension is gone; the excitement is spent; the anticipation is lost. If you must talk out your thoughts on the subject, talk them out by writing them down on paper as the ideas come to you.

In short, turn inward. Save yourself for your paper. Any creation by an artist has a life of its own, but it must first draw its life from the artist who creates it. To the extent that you use up your own life force in mundane matters during this week, to that extent you will be denying your artistic creation that which it has a right to expect from you: your total energy, your total being.

During this week you will find phrases and fragments of sentences forming in your mind. Whole sentences will come to you. Several good topic sentences will occur to you. When these flashes of insight come, write them down. Afterward, return to whatever you were doing when you thought of them. Keep a pad of paper by your bedside and when you awaken in the night with one of these flashes, write it down. If you wait until morning, you will have forgotten it. An outline will begin, gradually, to form in your mind, as you begin to integrate the material, as you live with it, as you make it a part of you.

I know that you still have your duties to perform. However, you will find that very little energy is required to move mechanically through those duties, and even less of your creative mind. Try percolating profitably for one week. If you succeed, I promise you that by the end of that week you will be aching to sit down at the typewriter and start writing. The results will be worth the effort.

The practical use: the outline

What about the practical use of this percolating week? I have said that an outline will begin to take shape in your mind, but what is an outline? Furthermore, how detailed should you expect it to be?

An outline evolves out of your theme and, in turn, defines and limits your theme. It grows from and reflects the organization and scope of your note cards. An outline keeps you from going off on tangents when you are writing. An outline also keeps the different parts of your paper in proportion. An outline, however, should never be allowed to have total control over your writing. Often, as you write, you will find your paper taking a twist you could not have foreseen. Evaluating the artistic and historical merit of that twist is an art in itself. Until practice teaches you that art, I recommend that you stay with your outline.

Any piece of scholarly writing is composed of four parts: (1) The introduction, wherein you tell the reader what you intend to write about. You state your hypothesis, or thesis, the theme that you intend to investigate and analyze. (2) The body of the paper, which contains all the evidence you have gathered on your theme, both pro and con. (3) The summary, wherein you review for the reader the evidence you have presented at length in the body of the paper. (4) The conclusions, which evolve from the evidence you have presented, together with your commentary.

Each of these four parts must be kept in balance with the whole. A rule of thumb to follow is: introduction, five percent; body, eighty percent; summary, five percent; conclusions and commentary, ten percent. Some leeway exists in this ratio. For your first paper, however, try to stay within these guidelines.

How detailed should your outline be? The key to use here is, how long should your paper be? This question is the inevitable one whenever a professor assigns a term paper. The answer he will give is, "As long as it takes you to say what you have to say." He will then add, "Not more than X pages." For your first paper, the number of pages he will most likely stipulate is thirty. This maximum number of pages, therefore, will be your guide in developing your outline.

If the body of your paper is to be no more than eighty percent, or twenty-four pages, your outline cannot be too detailed. You must cover two main topics, Cromwell (who, what, when, where) and the Tender of Union (what, when, where, whence), the historical setting, and the years you are including, which would be from at least 1649 (the execution of Charles I) through 1658 (Cromwell's death). Indeed, if Cromwell had made only one statement a year from 1651 through 1658 and you were to place that statement in its historical setting, you would be filling eight pages with this one topic alone (estimating approximately one page for each statement). If you require five pages at the beginning of the body of your paper to describe the historical setting of your topic, two pages to describe Cromwell, and two pages to describe the Tender, you will be using up an additional nine pages. Thus far you will have used a minimum of seventeen of your allotted twenty-four pages. If, in addition, you wish to have a section on the historiography of the subject, you must estimate the number of pages this section will require. If you have read ten books and six articles from which you wish to cite and you estimate one-half page for each of these authors, you will need an additional eight pages. You will have reached the maximum number allowed. I am not saying that you will require this number of pages for each section. I am demonstrating only that this pragmatic estimation is a good method to use when you are determining how involved you should let your outline become.

The outline I have described would look like this:

A. Introduction (½ page).
B. The historical setting of the Tender of Union (5 pages).
   1. Cromwell defined (2 pages).
   2. The Tender defined (2 pages).

c. Cromwell on the Tender (8 pages).
1. His references to it, from 1650 to 1658.
2. Together with historical setting for each reference (briefly).
d. The historiography of the subject (8 pages).
1. His contemporaries: friends and foes.
2. Historians of the 18th century (if you found any).
3. Historians of the 19th century (e.g., Carlyle).
4. Historians of the 20th century, to World War II.
5. Historians of the 20th century, since World War II.
e. Summary (1½ pages).
1. Of Cromwell's statements.
2. Of the leading historians.
f. My own conclusions (3 pages).

Beside each section you have written the maximum number of pages that you will be able to devote to that section and yet stay within the total maximum number of pages the professor has stipulated.

This outline is not the only approach you could take to the topic. However, it is the simplest and most manageable one. It is chronological within one topic and it keeps the focus on Cromwell.

Maintaining focus: the working title

The most demanding task in the completion of a research paper is that of maintaining focus. It is a task that begins with your outline and ends only when you have finished typing your final draft. This task can be well begun by formulating a working title, writing it at the head of your outline, and then checking that outline, unit by unit, to determine whether title and outline agree with one another in every detail. The working

title must justify the outline, just as the outline must ful-
fill the promise of the working title. In other words, they
must balance each other; they must agree.

A working title may be very long, somewhat like an
old-fashioned doctoral dissertation title. In fact, it
should be long because the more detail you include in it,
the more you will be delimiting the subject matter to be
included in the paper itself.

The working title will not be the title of the finished
paper. The outline I have suggested here could very
well have as its finished title, "Cromwell on the Union of
Scotland with England." A working title for the same
outline could read, "Cromwell's opinions on the union
of Scotland with England, taken from his own speeches
and writings, and the historiography of the subject selected from the writings of his contemporaries and from
the writings of selected historians down to the post
World War II period."

If, however, you found that your interest and reading had veered off to another direction, then both working title and outline must reflect that new direction. If
you would rather write on the subject of the opinions of
leading English parliamentarians and of the Scots to the
Tender of Union, in addition to Cromwell's, then the
"D" section of the outline would not deal with historiography, but with those different opinions of Cromwell's contemporaries. In this case the emphasis would
be on the Tender of Union itself, rather than on Cromwell, and a possible working title would be, "The opinions of the leading English parliamentarians of the
Long Parliament, of the Scots (writers, magistrates, or
church leaders—if you so delimited them), and of
Oliver Cromwell on the subject of the 1652 union of
Scotland with England."

The formulation of a working title is not merely

busy work. It forces the writer to reduce his whole paper to one sentence fragment. It forces him to focus on his topic; the outline that elaborates upon the promise in the working title forces him to maintain that focus. The writer thus avoids outlining a paper that has no theme; he avoids writing an open-end paper; he avoids going off on a tangent.

By the time this week of percolating draws to a close you will have a good idea of the form your paper will take. The concentration of thought that is necessary to formulate the working title and the outline will work co-operatively with the inward-turning process to prepare you for the task of creation. These necessary steps— particularly the estimation of the number of pages you will need for each section of the outline—will be difficult at first. They will become easier with each paper you do, as you develop your own style of expression and master the art of writing.

9

Write:

The Speaker Is Yourself (*Week 9*)

Good writing is clear writing. As a student you have come across much bad writing in the course of your reading. Bad writing is easy to recognize. Writing is bad when you do not understand what the writer is trying to say. This criterion applies only when you are reading in your own area of competence, however. If, as a student-historian, you cannot understand the text of a book on medicine, do not blame the author. You are not competent to pass judgment on his writing because you do not understand the technical language of the discipline.

The historian who writes well writes plain English, standard English, and avoids jargon and slang. He begins by learning how to write a good simple declarative English sentence. After he has mastered that art he may go on to write a compound sentence, but only after he has mastered the fundamentals of sentence construction. If you are unsure of yourself in this matter, stay with simple sentences. If you find yourself writing a sentence you cannot end, break down the sentence into its component ideas and start over again with several simple sentences in place of the cumbersome one. During Week 11, when you start to edit and rewrite, you will undoubtedly find many cumbersome sentences in your manuscript. You may not recognize them now while you are writing.

What is good essay form?

The paper you are writing is a formal essay. An essay is an analytical composition in which the pros and cons of an argument are weighed; a formal essay is one that is written in the third person.

An essay has a beginning, a middle, and an end. That sentence may appear silly; nevertheless, think about it. How many essays have you written in class, and at home, that have lacked a beginning, or an end? How many have you written that have been all beginning and no middle? The typical classroom essay is a case of the latter. A good beginning introduces the subject of the essay, as briefly as possible. A good ending sums up and concludes, again, as briefly as possible. A good essay answers all the interrogative pronouns, who, what, when, where, whence (how come?), and whither (so what?), in the middle. To the extent that you fail to answer any of these pronouns, to that extent you will have failed to write a good essay. A good essay answers the pronoun "why" only at the end, because the why of any historical question is always the historian's own conclusion. A good essay is structured, can be outlined easily because it was written from an outline, avoids tangents, and is devoid of emotional language.

A good essay is written in well-formed paragraphs. Each paragraph is formed by the elaboration of one idea, or by the elaboration of more than one idea when the ideas are closely related.

A good essay is one in which every paragraph begins with a topic sentence. A topic sentence tells your reader what the paragraph will be about. Indeed, you can learn the contents of a well-written essay, or book, merely by reading the topic sentences of every paragraph.

A good essay is one in which every paragraph evolves out of the paragraph that preceded it; that is, the ideas in a good essay will flow smoothly.

A good essay is one that is written with nouns and verbs and a minimum of adjectives and adverbs. It is one in which English word order dominates. English word order is: subject, verb, object, e.g., "Cromwell captured Edinburgh."

A good essay is written with the active voice dominating. Do not write, "Edinburgh was captured by Cromwell." Active voice has more dramatic force, is easier to write, and is easier to understand.

Finally, a good essay is an honest essay. An honest essay is one that contains no hot air, no waffling, no padding, no attempts to substitute meaningless words merely to fill the required number of pages. If you cannot write the full thirty pages, do not attempt to do so. Say what you have to say and stop. Your professor will appreciate the honesty in your writing, even though he will probably add that if you had done your research well you would have had no difficulty in filling thirty pages. Indeed, if you *have* done your research well, your problem will be to say what you have to say in *only* thirty pages. The self-discipline necessary in facing this problem is essential to learning how to write well. You will learn to make every word count.*

* See William Strunk, Jr. and E. B. White, *The Elements of Style,* 2nd edition (New York: Macmillan, 1972), 78 pages, for a concise statement of basic rules of grammar and punctuation, of the most common errors in writing, and of the rules basic to style.

What is a good history essay?

A good history essay is written in the third person. In this informal handbook I have used "I" and "you" because I am talking directly to you, telling you my conclusions and opinions on certain topics. In classroom essays and research papers, however, the historian never uses this style. In a formal essay he will not write, "You can understand why Cromwell acted as he did," as if he were talking informally to a class of students. He will write instead, "One can understand why Cromwell acted as he did." In a formal essay he will not write, "I think that Cromwell hated the Scots," but rather, "Cromwell hated the Scots." The historian keeps himself out of the story.

A good historical essay does not express an opinion or a conclusion as a fact. In the last example, "Cromwell hated the Scots," the writer (who is not an historian) is doing just that. The student-historian, aware of the distinction, would probably write instead, "Judging by his actions, Cromwell appears to have hated the Scots." The professional historian would undoubtedly modify the statement even further: "Judging by his actions, Cromwell's attitude toward the Scots was ambivalent. On the one hand, he . . ." This style of writing, which irritates many undergraduate students who would like simple answers, is the result of much study and much thought. The historian writes as he does, not because he does not know the answer, but rather because he knows that no one answer is adequate. A layman may dismiss Cromwell by saying simply, "He was a dictator." The historian may not.

The historian cites his sources in an essay. He cites every quotation, every paraphrase of a quotation, and any theory that is peculiar to a particular historian. To fail to cite one's sources is to try to pass off the words and ideas of another as one's own. To fail to cite one's sources is to be dishonest with the reader.

In the historical essay the footnotes will be of two kinds: (1) a simple citation of the source, and (2) substantive, or content notes. Two schools of thought exist on the subject of substantive footnotes. One school says that if the thought is worth putting in the paper at all, it belongs in the text. The other school says that any thought that would interrupt the smooth telling of the story by being put in the text should be put in a footnote instead. I prefer the second school; your professor, however, may not like content footnotes. I suggest that you ask him his preference in this matter.

The historian does not prove something

When a lawyer makes his summarizing statement before the jury, he is in fact composing an essay. A lawyer, however, is given much leeway in the words he may choose, in the tone of his voice, in the interpretation he wishes to give to the evidence, and even in the evidence he may choose to omit in that summation. The opposing lawyer is given the same leeway.

The historian is not given this leeway. His job is neither to defend nor to prosecute the person, or the situation, or the event he is writing about. The historian's job is to present the facts, all those that he has uncovered, omitting none that are important to his presentation. Indeed, learning to distinguish between the facts that are important and those that are unimportant is one of the historian's arts. His job is to choose his words with such care that they do not reveal his biases. He may not interpret the evidence to suit his fancy, not in the body of the paper, at least. In his conclusions the historian may interpret as he wishes; the reader, however, is free to disagree with him if the evidence he has presented does not substantiate those conclusions.

Your reader, your professor, is your judge and jury. You would like him to agree with you. However, even if he cannot agree with you, you do not want to give him any basis on which he can destroy your conclusions. Therefore, if you find yourself putting forth your own conclusions and none of the authorities agrees with you, make sure that those conclusions can be substantiated by the evidence you have presented in the body of your paper.

Finally, the historian does not omit evidence he does not agree with. Do not try to do so. The professor knows more about the subject than you; he will spot the omissions. You will be guilty of intellectual dishonesty. Whenever anyone does this, he is not thinking historically.

The setting

If you can possibly arrange matters so, do all your writing at the same desk in a room alone, preferably with the door shut and a "Do not disturb" sign on it. If this requirement causes an inconvenience to your spouse or roommate, work out a reciprocity agreement in advance. The inconvenience, after all, will be for only four to five hours a day and for only one week.

Writing is best done in the morning, when you are still relaxed and before the tensions of the day and the impact of encounters with others have fragmented your thoughts. If your schedule does not permit this luxury and you must write later in the day, try to set aside the same hours every day. Your writing will be of a more even quality as a result.

You cannot do creative, professional writing with the TV, radio, or stereo blaring, no matter how you may have studied when you were an undergraduate. Creative work demands no distractions, either conscious or subliminal. For one week you are to concentrate on one goal: saying what you have to say as well as you are able to say it.

Two approaches to writing

Two theories exist on the problem of starting to write. One theory counsels you to put something, anything, on paper, just as long as you start. The hypothesis is that you can rewrite later. The other theory counsels you to do the best job of writing that you can do on the very first draft.

The approach you use will depend largely on the use you made of the week that has just passed. If you have not percolated in a productive way, you will find that you *have* to resort to the first; your thoughts will not be sufficiently integrated to attempt the second approach. If, on the other hand, you have percolated profitably, you will be *able* to use the second approach; the material will be so much a part of your thoughts that your sentences and paragraphs will form themselves without difficulty.

The first approach is a messy one; no job is harder than that of trying to rewrite a badly organized paragraph or a poorly constructed sentence. I recommend that you do the best you can on the first draft. You will save time later, when you edit.

Rules the professional uses

The average professional writer writes five pages a day. The average undergraduate tries to write a twenty-page term paper in one night. As a student-historian, which person do you want to emulate? If you average one acceptable page of typescript an hour and work five hours each day, you will have your paper done in six days.

Set a limit on your writing period. Do not drag it out. Tell yourself that you will spend five hours a day writing five pages of typescript a day for six days. Having set this time limit, stick to it. I had a creative writing teacher who told us that writing and finishing that which we began was only a matter of self-discipline, that inspiration was not involved. "You cannot wait until the lilacs bloom before you begin to write," she would say. You cannot wait until the muse visits you; you must call her to your side and keep her there.

Each evening go over the outline and estimate what portion of it you will be able to write up the following day. You can do this by reviewing the notes that cover the next portion of the outline and by inserting in the outline all the pertinent details that the notes reveal. You are now making an expanded outline. Then estimate the *minimum* number of lines you will need to write up each of those details. Write your estimation on your expanded outline: "one sentence," "half a page," "2–3 sentences." When your estimation totals five pages, you will have sliced off that portion of your outline that you will be able to write up the next day. When you are writing the next day, stay within the estimation. By disciplining yourself to do so you will sharpen your ability to use words economically.

When you are writing the next day, do not go beyond the portion you have assigned for yourself for that day, even if you know exactly what you intend to say. Do not write yourself out in any one day. If you do, you will run the risk of overdoing one day and then of being too tired to write the next day. A good place to stop is immediately after you have written the topic sentence for the first paragraph of the next day's section.

A trick that many professional writers use is to write the topic sentence and *part* of the second sentence, and to leave the paper in the typewriter with the second sentence unfinished. I recommend this trick; it works. If you follow it you will find that when you sit down at the typewriter the next day, you will know what you wanted to say to finish the sentence. The act of finishing it will stimulate the third sentence into being and, thus, you are writing, without undergoing the amateur's agonizing over how to begin.

Write every day. Leave no time in between for your ideas to become cold. If necessary, play a game with yourself. Tell yourself that you will at least finish that second sentence and start the third. This trick works also. I have sat down at the typewriter on days when I was sure that I would not be able to turn out a decent sentence. Nevertheless, the act of sitting, of finishing that second sentence and, while I was there, of starting the third sentence and, that finished, of starting the fourth, has trapped me into many a five-hour stint at the typewriter. When I have done that, I am able to quit with a good feeling. Thus I avoid the nagging discomfort that follows having done something else when I should have been writing.

How to begin

All writers agonize over a beginning sentence; you are not alone. However, the straightforward opening sentence has yet to be improved upon. Do not aim for tricky phrasing or fancy words; do not try to make an impression. If I were writing this paper on Cromwell, my first sentence would be a plain declarative one, such as:

In the spring of 1652 the governor of Scotland proclaimed the union of Scotland and England in one commonwealth.

With this sentence out of the way, the remainder of the introduction follows easily. Remember only that the introduction must agree with the working title:

The man who had prime responsibility in effecting this union was Oliver Cromwell, the Governor of England. What the Tender of Union was, why it was, what Cromwell thought of it, and the interpretations that leading historians have placed upon his views—these are the topics that this essay will cover.

Straightforward; no gimmicks. You are ready to go into the body of the paper, into the historical setting for the union. You will probably write,

There are many reasons why the union was made.

You are on your way. Two weeks from now, when you are editing your paper, you may want to change your wording. For now, however, it stands as it is and, as it is, it serves its purpose: it got you started.

Some hints on the mechanics of the first draft

Type the first draft on cheap yellow typing paper; type the second draft on cheap white paper. This color device is helpful when someone disturbs the papers on your desk or when a sudden gust of wind sends everything flying.

Double space the first draft. Type on one side of the paper only. Set the margins to approximate those you will use on the final draft. Whenever you cite a source, put it in the first draft, and in full. You will be tempted to tell yourself that you will put it in later. If you do this, you will run the risk of forgetting where you wanted to cite. Even if you do remember, you will have to rummage through your cards looking for the right one. Type the citation at the exact place in the text from which you are referring. Type it in full, exactly as it will appear in the final draft. You will save time and energy later, when you are typing your final draft. An added bonus will be that when you type the final draft you will be able to achieve a more accurate estimate on how many lines you will have to leave at the bottom of each page for your citations.

Never copy another writer's footnote. To do this is not only dishonest, it is also self-defeating. You may be copying his mistake.

Do not assign numbers to the citations at this time. You do not yet know how many more citations you will insert when you edit and rewrite; neither do you know how many you will delete from the final draft. As long as the citation comes immediately after the sentence to which it refers, you do not need numbers. I set the citation off by placing it within parentheses. I ring the citations with red marking pen that same evening when I am reading over the day's script. By doing this, I am better able to reread the text and avoid the distraction of the notes. In this way I am better able to sense the flow of the text.

Do not worry about how messy your script may appear with all its corrections. You do not want to disturb the flow of your ideas or waste your energy by retyping merely so that you can have a clean page of typescript to admire. At the risk of sounding pedantic, I would say that you have not yet earned the right to admire it. Wait until it is finished. Continue writing; stay with the outline. If you must feel gratification at this stage, derive that gratification from the knowledge that each day you have sliced off another section of the outline and are finished with it.

10

Let It Cool Off:

Return to This World (*Week 10*)

IF YOU did your research methodically and consistently, and if you spent your percolating week actually percolating and not merely procrastinating, you were able to write your thirty-page paper in six days. Now you have earned the right to be proud of your accomplishment. Now you are entitled to a week off. Do not return your books to the library. You will undoubtedly need them next week when you return to your paper. Do not attempt to edit and rewrite during this week; it is still too fresh in your mind. You will not see your errors. Close up the folder. Put it away. Let it cool off. Return to this world.

Put the paper completely out of your mind. Use this week for anything else. Catch up on the duties you have been attending to in only a perfunctory way for the past two weeks. Look at the students in your classes and really see them again. Listen to what they are saying. Take your spouse to see that new movie. Indulge in a bull session or two in the students' lounge. Read the newspapers and catch up on the news. Watch the late show on TV. Relax. You have earned the right.

Toward the end of the week you will find yourself wondering what you *did* write in that paper. You will have forgotten; you will find yourself wanting to read it. When this urge comes, but not before, you are ready to edit and rewrite. Make yourself comfortable on the sofa, pencil in hand, and start reading. You will find yourself editing and rewriting before you realize it.

11

Edit and Rewrite:

Be Your Own Best Enemy (*Week 11*)

Be your own best enemy. Who is your best enemy? He is the person who tells you your faults and does not mind hurting you as he does so. He may really be your most annoying friend in disguise.

Read your paper in as detached a manner as you possibly can. Pretend that someone else has written it and that you are being paid to find fault with it. Pretend also that you are being paid to recognize and praise its good points. In short, be objective.

A checklist for your text: first reading

As you read your paper the first time, do not concern yourself with content. With as many errors in style as the paper undoubtedly contains, you cannot begin to evaluate its content; poor style obscures the value of its content.

The average student does not know how to edit his first draft because he does not recognize everything that is wrong with it. Even if you are not a gifted writer, however, your paper will be improved if you will delete its most glaring errors. The list that follows constitutes the most common errors. Use this list as you read your paper. Make all necessary changes.

1. Delete all references to "I," "you," "we," and "us."
2. Delete all slang expressions and colloquialisms.
3. Delete all contractions: "won't," "can't." Write out "will not" and "cannot."
4. Delete all cliches: "adding fuel to the fire"; "hoisted by his own petard"; "Be that as it may. . . ." Rewrite.
5. Correct all sentences where you have used "like" as a conjunction. "Like" is a preposition; the conjunction is "as." Examples: "The Scots were not *like* the English," but "The Scots acted *as* they did because. . . ."
6. Delete all quotation marks that you put in only for effect. That is, do not call attention to a colloquialism or a piece of slang by putting quotation marks around it. Use quotation marks only when you are inserting a quote in the body of your paragraph.
7. Delete all uses of "etc.," "and so forth," and "and many more." They are the mark of the amateur.
8. Write out in full all words that you have abbreviated.
9. Delete all uses of the conjunctions "and" or "but" at the beginning of sentences.
10. If you must use a connective, make use of the rich collection that English provides: nevertheless, however, notwithstanding, moreover, no doubt.
11. Correct all misuses of the conjunction "but." "But" is used in contrasting two equal statements: "Leslie was powerful, but not so powerful as Cromwell." Compare these two sentences: (1) "Leslie was powerful, but still he had to yield"; (2) "Leslie was pow-

erful; nevertheless, he had to yield." The second sentence uses a connecting adverb, and therefore conveys your meaning more precisely.

12. Delete all uses of the adjective "great" unless you are describing something tangible that is mammoth in size. Do not use it as a substitute for the precise adjective. Used thus, it is the mark of a lazy mind. Use Roget's *Thesaurus* * or a book of synonyms to find the exact word you want to use.

13. Correct all spelling errors. If you are in doubt about the spelling of a word, you have probably misspelled it. Look it up in a dictionary.

14. Correct all punctuation. As a general rule, avoid the use of dashes. Learn the basic uses of the colon, the semicolon, and the comma. Be sure that you have not connected two independent sentences by the use of a comma. Separate them by the use of a period or a semicolon instead.

A checklist for your text: second reading

On the same evening read your paper through again. On the second reading you will still be concerned primarily with style. A second concern, although a minor one, will be its content.

15. Change all unnecessary uses of the passive voice to the active voice.

16. Check all your adjectives, one by one. Is each one necessary? Does it add substance to your statement? Could you delete it and strengthen the statement by choosing a more dramatic verb instead?

* Roget, Peter Mark, *The Original Roget's Thesaurus of English Words and Phrases,* new edition, Robert A. Dutch, editor (New York: St. Martin's Press, 1964), 1405 pages.

17. Check your adjectives and verbs for their neutrality. Have you written any biased ones? If you have, neutralize them.
18. Check your precision. Have you chosen the precise noun and verb or have you allowed yourself to be lazy and use the first word that came to mind.
19. Check your conciseness. Have you put in unnecessary words and phrases just to pad out the paper, or because you like the sound they make, or because you hope they will impress the professor? Delete all unnecessary words.

Type a second draft

At the end of the second reading the corrections will have made a mess of your manuscript. The question will now be, how well do you type? Any serious student should learn to type proficiently. If he does not, he will spend too much money on commercial typists. If he does not, he will try to avoid typing a second draft. He will try to go directly from a corrected first draft to a finished one. The results will not be good. You cannot recognize all the errors that remain to be corrected when you are working from a messy script.

At this point in your editing you should retype the paper in full. If you can type five pages an hour, allot three hours an evening for two evenings and type a clean copy, incorporating all your corrections thus far.

A checklist for your text: third reading

On the fourth evening of the week of editing and rewriting you will be working from a clean draft. Staple together the pages of the first draft and keep it. A professor will question the authorship of a paper whose caliber does not agree with his impression of the student's ability. He may ask to see all earlier drafts. If the student cannot produce them, he cannot substantiate his authorship.

On the fourth evening of editing your concern will still be with style, but primarily with content. Six points need to be checked this evening:

20. Does each paragraph begin with a topic sentence?
21. Does each paragraph consist of an elaboration of that topic sentence, and that only?
22. Does each paragraph flow from the paragraph that preceded it? If it does not, you may have written a substantive footnote into the body of your paper.
23. Does your introductory paragraph for the paper as a whole introduce the reader to the topic as a whole?
24. Does your summarizing section summarize the body of the essay, or have you strayed off into writing conclusions?
25. Do your conclusions evolve from the body of the paper? Are they substantiated by the evidence that you presented in the body, or have you gone off on a tangent?

A checklist for your text: fourth reading

After you have read through the paper and have made all the corrections that these twenty-five points have called to your attention, you will be ready to read it for content only.

Two questions are important for this reading: (1) What is necessary to the telling of the story and what is unnecessary? (2) Is any sentence, or part of a sentence, ambiguous?

Examine each paragraph individually. Ask yourself, without this paragraph would the paper still make sense? Would the evidence in the following paragraph flow smoothly from the preceding paragraph if I were to delete this one? If the story *would* flow smoothly, that paragraph may be unnecessary. Ask yourself, in my summary and conclusions have I made use of the thread of this particular paragraph? If you have not, either your summary and conclusions are wanting or the paragraph *is* unnecessary. If it is unnecessary, delete it.

Cutting is painful. One difference between the amateur and the professional writer, however, is that the professional is not afraid to cut words, sentences, paragraphs, or whole pages, when the story will be improved by so doing. The amateur avoids cutting; he thinks that every word he has written is priceless. You are in training to become a professional. Start now. Cut when cutting will improve the story.

Examine each sentence of each paragraph for possible ambiguity. Do you have any pronoun with an unclear antecedent acting as the subject of a sentence? I am not returning to a study of syntax; I am referring to contents as they reflect the clarity of your thinking. Often a writer will find that his contents are not clear once he begins to eliminate this last, most grievous, error. The contents will not be clear because his thinking has not been clear.

As you read your paper the fourth time, on the fourth evening, you will find ambiguity in the opening paragraph:

In the spring of 1652 the Governor of Scotland proclaimed the union of Scotland and England in one commonwealth. The man who had prime responsibility in effecting this union was Oliver Cromwell, the Governor of England. What the

Tender of Union was, why it was, what Cromwell thought of it, and the interpretations that leading historians have placed upon his views— these are the topics that this essay will cover.

The first two sentences are all right. The third sentence, however, is cumbersome; it does not end gracefully. English word order has been inverted. That inversion has made necessary the use of an unclear pronoun, "these," acting as the subject of the sentence. The sentence must be rewritten.

Begin with the subject of the sentence, "topics," and the sentence will clarify:

The topics that this paper will cover include a description of the historical setting of the Tender of Union, an analysis of the contents of the Tender, a description of Cromwell's position in the English government, his views on the Union, and the interpretations that leading historians have placed upon those views.

Having been alerted to unclear pronouns acting as subjects, you will notice that the first sentence of your paragraph on the historical setting must be rewritten also. As you have written it, it reads:

There are many reasons why the Union was made.

In order to understand why this sentence is bad you must parse it. The subject is "reasons." Rewrite the sentence, starting with the subject:

Many reasons are (why the Union was made).

Now that you have placed the subject first, you have uncovered your use of the least descriptive of all verbs, "are." It is the lazy writer's verb. What more descriptive verb could you substitute? "Coalesced," "converged," "existed," "lay behind," "went into," "entered into," "played a part," "were operating," are a few of the choices you have. If you do not have a wide choice of verbs at your command, use your book of synonyms or your Roget's *Thesaurus*. Choose a more descriptive verb and rewrite the sentence.

On this fourth evening reread your paper with this goal in mind, ferreting out and changing all sentences that begin with unclear subjects, such as:

> There are many . . .
> It is obvious that . . .
> It seemed as if . . .
> This is the reason why . . .
> This (that) is why . . .

In each case, ask yourself: What does "There" stand for? What do I mean by "It"? "This" what? The last two sentences are easiest of all to correct. You need only place the noun after "This" and before "is," or else re-word the sentence to read, "For this reason, . . ."

Editing is hard work. It demands objectivity. It demands the willingness to read and reread and read again, to delete, and to rewrite. Nevertheless, this hard work will pay off, I promise you, in the quality of your finished work.

As you learn to make yourself conscious of errors *as you are making them* and as you discipline yourself not to let those errors enter into the first draft, your writing will improve on the first draft. As the quality of your writing improves on the first draft, the time, effort, and pain involved in editing and rewriting will lessen. Let that bright promise stir you to do your best work the first time. If you will so train yourself, you will find that you will begin to enjoy the challenge of writing. We all enjoy doing that which we do well.

12

Your Paper Is Done:

Only Clerical Details Remain (*Week 12*)

TYPING the final draft calls for more self-discipline. Occasionally, you will find an error that you had not spotted earlier. When this happens, correct it. However, do not let yourself stray from your corrected second draft by trying to write in any last-minute thoughts you may have on the subject. If you have edited as I have suggested, these last-minute additions would not dovetail with the rest of the paper. They would, in fact, detract from the paper. In addition, last-minute thoughts are rarely brilliant. Type from your second draft as you have edited it.

Typing the final draft

If your department or college has a manual for term paper format, study and follow it. If none is available, the following suggestions represent a standard form. Use sixteen or twenty pound paper that has cotton content because paper with cotton content is easier to erase. If your professor does not object to erasable paper, use it. Short cuts are useful in clerical matters.

Clean the typewriter keys before you start typing.

Make sure the ribbon is dark enough to permit the paper to be read easily.

You will either collect the footnotes at the bottom of each page or you will make back notes of them by putting them at the end of the paper. Ask the professor which form he prefers. Now is the time to number the footnotes. Number them consecutively throughout the paper.

Set the typewriter margins: one and one-quarter inches on the left and one inch on the right. The bottom margin should be one inch from the bottom of the page. Make a pencil mark on the paper to act as a guide. Then count off the number of lines you will need at the bottom for the footnotes, estimating five lines to the inch. If you will need five lines for footnotes, make a pencil mark at least two and one-half inches from the bottom of the page, thus allowing one inch for the footnotes, one inch for the bottom margin, and half an inch for a dividing space between the text and the footnotes.

Begin the first page by centering the title on the ninth or tenth line down from the top of the page. Type the title in capital letters. Do not underline it. Begin the paper three or four lines down from the title. Indent each paragraph by spacing in five letters. Double-space the text. When you come to the end of a page of typescript, separate the text from the footnotes by double-spacing and then making a line of ten or twenty spaces with the underlining key (over the number 6 on the keyboard). Indent the first line of each footnote by five spaces. Type the number of the footnote in superscript, that is, half a space up from the line of type. Type the footnote in single space: *

* For examples of different footnote forms, consult either Kate L. Turabian, *A Manual for Writers of Term Papers, Theses, and Dissertations,* 3rd edition (Chicago: University of Chicago Press, 1967), 164

¹ Wilbur Cortez Abbott, *A Bibliography of Oliver Cromwell; a list of printed materials relating to Oliver Cromwell; together with a list of portraits and caricatures* (Cambridge, Mass.: Harvard University Press, 1929), p. 186.

Begin the second and each succeeding page by writing the number of the page in the upper right corner of the page one inch from the right side and seven spaces down from the top of the paper. Three lines beneath this number, continue with the text.

Compiling the printed bibliography

After your professor has read the title of your paper, he will turn to your printed bibliography. A student will avoid being suspected of intellectual dishonesty by including in his bibliography *only* those books and articles he has cited in his paper. If you wish to let the professor know that you have consulted other works as well, divide the bibliography in two parts. Call the first part, BIBLIOGRAPHY OF WORKS CITED. Call the second part, ADDITIONAL REFERENCES CONSULTED.

Arrange your 3-by-5 bibliography cards according to the kind of source each card represents: primary; secondary, books; secondary, articles. Within each of these three categories, arrange your cards by author or editor. You are ready to type your bibliography. You will be glad now that you took complete bibliographic notes at the beginning of your project. All you have to do is copy the information from each card:

Abbott, Wilbur Cortez. *A Bibliography of Oliver Cromwell; a list of printed materials relating to*

pages, or Peyton Hurt, *Bibliography and Footnotes: A Style Manual for Students,* 3rd edition revised (Berkeley, Calif.: University of California Press, 1968), 163 pages.

> *Oliver Cromwell; together with a list of portraits and caricatures.* Cambridge, Mass.: Harvard University Press, 1929. 551 pages.

Include the number of pages in the book, or the number of volumes in the set, so that if you should include a book the professor is not familiar with, he will be able to use the number of pages you list as a fast way (although not the only way) of evaluating the worth of the book.

Under the first part, BIBLIOGRAPHY OF WORKS CITED, list your cited sources in the following order under the following subheadings: *Primary Sources; Secondary Sources: Books;* and *Journal Articles.*

After you have finished typing the paper, proofread it. Your spouse can help with this job. Have her (or him) hold the copy of the final draft while you read aloud from the corrected second draft. Make corrections neatly. Ink corrections are usually permitted on a term paper, but never on a thesis.

Make a copy for yourself

Before you hand in your paper, have a copy made for yourself. Whatever you write is and remains your property (unless you sell the rights to it). Your professor is morally and legally obligated to return the paper to you unless he has stipulated in advance that he will not do so. If he has said this, then the obligation to make a copy for yourself *before you hand it in* falls upon you.

What about after you have handed it in?

What do you do with all those 3-by-5 bibliography cards? with those 5-by-8 note cards? with those two drafts and the copy of the final paper?

File them away for future reference. Arrange your

3-by-5 bibliography cards into an author-subject card catalog, alphabetically by author or editor, primary and secondary sources interfiled. Write the generic heading "On Cromwell" on one of your dividing cards. Do the same with the 5-by-8 note cards. Remove them from their compartments and, in the same order in which you used them, place them all together in one compartment of your file box under the generic heading "On Cromwell." File the two drafts of the paper together with the copy of the final paper in a manila folder in your 9-by-12 file box.

Later, you will be glad that you attended to these minor clerical details now. You will be able to use those cards and notes to review for your comprehensive exams.

After you have done this, spend a few minutes thinking over the past twelve weeks. What would you do differently next time? If you went wrong somewhere, where was it? Use the inside covers of this handbook to make a few notes to yourself. Do not rely on your memory; it is a poor witness.

*   *   *

Dear student: If I have laid down fast rules for you to follow, I have done so because both you and your professor will respond favorably to a research paper that gives evidence of having been prepared with careful attention to the trifles that make perfection. Your professor's response will show in the grade he gives you. Your response will consist in the gratification that comes only from a job well done.

That attention to trifles begins with your first trip to the library and ends only with your last trip to the seminar room. My aim in writing this handbook has been to map the road that lies between, to light up the dark places, to recommend a safe speed limit, and to post the danger signs, in short, to make that road less hazardous to travel. If you experience a sense of satisfaction when you finish your journey, I shall have achieved that aim.

Appendix

The Student's Home Reference Shelf

On the Historical Method

Jacques Barzun and Henry F. Graff, *The Modern Researcher*, revised edition (New York: Harcourt, Brace & World, 1970), 430 pages. Paper, $3.45.

Bibliographic Reference Source

Helen J. Poulton, *The Historian's Handbook: A Descriptive Guide to Reference Works* (Norman, Okla.: University of Oklahoma Press, 1972), 304 pages. Paper, $4.95.

Nonbibliographic Reference Sources

Columbia Encyclopedia, 3rd edition, William Bridgwater and Seymour Kurtz, eds. (New York: Columbia University Press, 1963), 2388 pages. $49.50.

William L. Langer, ed., *An Encyclopedia of World History: Ancient, Medieval, and Modern, Chronologically Arranged,* 5th edition (Boston: Houghton Mifflin, 1972), 1504 pages. $17.50.

Clifford L. Lord and Elizabeth H. Lord, *Historical Atlas of the United States,* revised edition (New York: Holt, 1953), 238 pages. Johnson reprint, 1969. $15.00.

Richard B. Morris and Henry S. Commager, eds., *En-*

cyclopedia of American History, revised and enlarged edition (New York: Harper, 1970), 840 pages. $12.50.

William R. Shepherd, *Shepherd's Historical Atlas*, 9th edition (New York: Barnes & Noble, 1964), 226 plus 115 pages. $17.50.

Webster's New Geographical Dictionary (Springfield, Mass.: G. & C. Merriam Co., 1973), 1408 pages. $14.95.

World Almanac and Book of Facts, published annually by different newspapers throughout the United States. Price varies.

Writing

A Manual of Style, 12th edition (Chicago: University of Chicago Press, 1969), 546 pages. $10.00.

Roget, Peter Mark, *The Original Roget's Thesaurus of English Words and Phrases*, new edition, Robert A. Dutch, editor (New York: St. Martin's Press, 1964), 1405 pages. $6.95.

William Strunk, Jr. and E. B. White, *The Elements of Style*, 2nd edition (New York: The Macmillan Co., 1972), 78 pages. Paper, $1.25.

Webster's Seventh New Collegiate Dictionary, based on *Webster's Third New International Dictionary* (Springfield, Mass.: G. & C. Merriam Co., 1972), 1221 pages. $6.95.

Footnote and Bibliography Forms

Peyton Hurt, *Bibliography and Footnotes: A Style Manual for Students and Writers*, 3rd edition, revised and enlarged by Mary L. Hurt Richmond (Berkeley: University of California Press, 1968), 163 pages. Paper, $2.25.

Kate L. Turabian, *A Manual for Writers of Term Papers, Theses, and Dissertations*, third edition, revised (Chicago: University of Chicago Press, 1967), 164 pages. Paper, $1.25.

Index